REMNANT

Dr. Charles Kriessman

Disclaimer

The author of this work has quoted the writers of many articles and books. This does not mean that the author endorses or recommends the works of others. If the author quotes someone, it does not mean that he agrees with all of the author's tenets, statements, concepts, or words, whether in the work quoted or any other work of the author. There has been no attempt to alter the meaning of the quotes; and therefore, some of the quotes are long in order to give the entire sense of the passage.

Address All Inquiries To:
THE OLD PATHS PUBLICATIONS, Inc.
142 Gold Flume Way
Cleveland, Georgia, U.S.A.

Web: www.theoldpathspublications.com
E-mail: TOP@theoldpathspublications.com

DEDICATION

This book is dedicated to all Jews in Israel. It is a plea for them to realize that the Lord Jesus Christ is their Redeemer and Messiah. If it becomes too late and the Rapture has come and gone, the prayer is for all Israel to respond to the everlasting gospel and be preserved until the Messiah brings you into the Kingdom. This book is for you.

TABLE OF CONTENTS

DEFINED TERMS

Abrahamic Covenant – An eternal unconditional set of promises given by God to Abraham in Genesis 12: 1-3. God gave Abraham and all his descendants the land which will become Israel forever, make the Jewish nation great, and bless those who bless Israel.

Abomination of Desolation – A mid-70th week event or forty-two months after the Antichrist signs a peace treaty with Israel; (David 9:27). The daily sacrifice in the Temple will be replaced with a speaking image of Antichrist which will be commanded to be worshipped as God or be killed.

Accommodation – This is theological compromise. It is the departure from doctrinal truth and unity for some higher cause or purpose. When believers join in a ministry effort with either an unbeliever or another believer, who are in violation of obedience to God's words, that is accommodation.

Antichrist – Future leader of the world who makes a peach agreement with Israel then breaks it three and one-half years into the Tribulation. He meets his end when he is defeated at Armageddon by the Lord Jesus Christ when he and the false prophet are both cast into the Lake of Fire. (Revelation 19:20)

Antisemitism – Hatred for the Jewish people.

Apostasy – From "apostasia" meaning to depart (fall away) from. It is a deliberate and complete abandonment of faith once delivered to the saints, (Jude 3), and a rejection of God.

Church – Those saved between the day of Pentecost (Acts 2) and Pre-Tribulation Rapture. Includes saved Jews and saved Gentiles. Those saints from before Pentecost and after the Rapture belong to other sheepfolds (John 10:1). There are distinctions between groups of saints in history: Old Testament saints, Church saints, Tribulation saints, and Millennial saints.

Covenant – A solemn agreement between groups or individuals . God made covenant with Israel as well as with Abraham, Adam, Noah, Moses, and David. Usually divided into conditional and unconditional covenants.

Day of the Lord – The time in the future that includes the seven-year Tribulation (Daniel's 70th week), and the entire one thousand year Millennium Kingdom.

Davidic Covenant – Found in 2 Samuel 7:12-17. This covenant reaffirms and extends God's covenant with Abraham. It is unconditional and together with the Abrahamic covenant makes up the basis for Israel's future existence, restoration, and the earthly kingdom.

Diaspora – The word means to scatter. The Diaspora of the Jews began for them in 70 A.D. (after several smaller ones), with the destruction of the Temple and Jerusalem. The Jews were cast out of their land (Matthew 24:2; Mark 13:2, Luke 21:6), and scattered throughout the nations for 1900 years. The Nation of Israel in the modern, latter days was reborn in 1948.

Dispensation(s) – Divisions of human history into periods of time whereby God has made Himself known, and continues to make himself known, revealing his eternal program and purposes as pertaining to mankind upon the earth. Knowledge of God's intentions enables one to know how to read and rightly divide the words of Truth. Dispensationalism distinguishes between Israel and the Church in God's plan. In every dispensation, genuine, personal faith in the person and work of Jesus Christ is always the means of salvation and relationship to God.

Doctrine – Teachings, what is taught, instruction. What is taught in the Bible.

Election – From the Greek, *"Ekloge,"* meaning the picked out ones, chosen, selected, that which is chosen by God. The source of this choosing is God's grace and not by the will of man.

Eschatological(y) – The study or science of last things; that is, end-time, latter-day events in connection with the current age. It is a word from the Greek, *"eschata,"* meaning the last things. It's context the doctrine of end-time events is contained mostly in the books of Daniel and Revelation. In this book the end-time or eschatological Jewish remnant refers to the called out Jews in Revelation 12, the middle of Daniel's 70th week. This book also adheres to the futurist theory of time which literally interprets the Bible and foresees revelation prophecy as yet to be fulfilled.

Firman – A near eastern sovereign's edict. A grant or permit.

Futurism – The orthodox view of eschatology. This is literal interpretation of literal events spanning the as yet to be fulfilled events of Revelation 6-20, and corresponding to the 70th week of Daniel.

Heptade – A sum or number of seven or groups of seven.

Heresy – From the Greek, *"hairesis,"* meaning a denial of revealed truth, causing destructive opinions.

Imagination – A mental image that is not real to the senses; assumptions, suppositions, conjectures, guesses; lies.

Messiah – From the Hebrew, *"Mesiha,"* which stands for the anointed one. Christ is the Greek word. Refers to the fact that Jesus Christ is the anointed of God, chosen to be the Lord and Saviour. The meaning for end-times is that Jesus Christ is the promised Messiah and that he will appear in the end-time.

Metaphor – A figure of speech containing an implied comparison in which a word of phrase ordinarily and primarily used of one thing is applied to another.

Millennium – The thousand year reign of Christ on earth.

New Covenant – (Luke 22:20; 1 Corinthians 11:25; 2 Corinthians 3:6; Hebrews 8:8,13; 9:15; 12:24). The new covenant replaced the Mosaic covenant and is God's promise of blessing to mankind through the Lord Jesus Christ. Christians share the spiritual benefits through Christ. Israel is promised eternal restoration as the head of all nations, their land, and a renewal of their hearts to obey God.

Second Coming – Jesus Christ told His disciples that He would go away and come back again to gather His own. (John 14:3). For dispensationalists it will be a two-phase event. Christ will come in the air (1Thessolonains 4:16) at the Pre-Tribulation Rapture and then at the end of the seven year Tribulation. He will come back with His saints to establish the Millennial Kingdom (Rev. 20: 11-15)

Replacement Theology – Supersessionism says that God is finished with Israel and that the Church inherits the promises and blessings and fulfills the Covenants that were once Israel's.

Remnant – Many words in the Bible translate remnant. They also are translated, "the rest", "remainder", "survivors", and "escaped". It is a technical biblical term which in many passages looks to the distant future of a "remnant" of Jewish souls who will be converted and receive the covenant blessings. "As the Lord hath said, and in the remnant whom the Lord shall call." (Joel 2:32; Isaiah 11:11). "Remnant" is an important doctrine running through the Old Testament and the New Testament. It affirms that no matter the horrific apostasy of Israel and God's judgment in "the Day of the Lord," a faithful Jewish remnant will exist to enter the Kingdom.

Secular – According to Webster; of or relating to the worldly or temporal. Not specifically religions, ecclesiastical, or clerical. Related to worldly things or definitions as separate from church or religious matters

Seignories – (san-ye-re,s). Noun, signifying power or authority of a feudal Lord; the territory over which a Lord holds jurisdiction. "Behold, I will stretch out mine hand upon the Philistines, and I will cut off the cherethims, and destroy the remnant of the sea cost." (Ezekiel 25:26)

Theology – From the Greek words, *"theos,"* meaning God, and *"logos"* meaning discourse or study. Theology is the study of God which is accomplished through a systematic study of the doctrines of God, his proof of existence, knowability, person, attributes, names, works, decree, and government.

Theonomist – Person who believes Old Testament law is still in effect today and should be followed. They usually adhere to an amillennial view of the Bible. John 1:17.

Tribulation – Period of 7 years known as Daniel's 70th week, the purpose of which is to judge the unbelieving peoples and nations of the earth (2 Thessalonians 2:12). It will also be left to God to deal with the nation of Israel (Daniel 9:24), two-third of the Jews of Israel will be killed by the Antichrist, while one-third of the

Jews are preserved as the eschatological remnant (Zechariah 13:8,9).

BIOGRAPHICAL PAGE

Charles Kriessman has been saved since the Lord called in on September 12, 1983. He attends the Bible for Today Church in Collingswood, New Jersey, via Internet Streaming, since 2004. Pastor D.A. Waite, Th.D., PH.D is the Pastor of BFT.

Charles was born in Washington, D.C., sixty-nine years ago. He has studied the subject of Bible Versions since 1985. He has written a book on the subject entitled "Modern Version Failures."

He has attended Gustavus Adolphus College in St Peter, Minnesota; Orange Coast College in Costa Mesa, California; and Macedonia Baptist College in Midland, North Carolina.

Mr. Kriessman currently holds a Doctorate Degree in Biblical Studies from G.C. B.I. in Ft. Walton Beach, Florida.

He is currently working on a doctorate Degree in theology from G.C.B.I. in Ft. Walton Beach, Florida.

INTRODUCTION

Let's get this out in the open and get this straight.

"Even so then at this present time also there is a remnant according to the election of grace. "(Romans 11:5)

There is no remnant in operation today, either Jewish or Christian. To state that there is such is in violation of God's rule for the remnant of Jews He has maintained throughout history.

When Paul penned Romans 11:5, he was referring to the remnant that was being preserved before the scattering after 70 A.D. It also refers to Chapter 11 as being Israel's future as God calls them out and restores the future of Israel in the coming kingdom. As for there being a Jewish remnant during the Church Age is not in view here. What is in view is the preserving and calling out of the remnant of Jews in the Tribulation and after the Tribulation. As to why there is no called out remnant present today between the Diaspora and the Tribulation will be dealt with in a later chapter.

This book is about the remnant, the eschatological, Jewish remnant which will be found in Revelation 12:17 as keeping God's revelation in the Tribulation "And the dragon was wroth with the woman, and went to make war with the remnant of her seed, which keep the commandments of God, and have the testimony of Jesus Christ. Besides the accepted meaning of obeying, this and many other passages containing the command of keeping God's words, echo the truth of the Great Commission that requires all believers to receive, preserve and obey God's oral and written revelation. [1]

The history of the Jewish remnant will be explored through the Scriptures. The thread of the remnant is found in the earliest Scriptures but is developed in certain Old Testament books such as Daniel and Isaiah. Remnant is translated by several Hebrew root words which is covered in the abstract.

Some Bible passages do not contain remnant terminology but is revealed through related concepts. One of these will be expounded in this book.

Perhaps it is needed to be realized that there is a strict doctrine of the remnant.

> *"Except the Lord of hosts had left us a very small remnant, we should have been as Sodom and we should have been like unto Gomorrah."* (Isaiah 1:9)

That is to say Israel would have been no more, just like Sodom and Gomorrah. God destroyed them around 1868 B.C and there hasn't been anything found of them since. Not that there has been any lack for trying. They are gone, wiped out, and the same was in store many times for Israel except that God watches out for them for His own sake.

So, the doctrine of the remnant, or the salvation of Israel as stated in the Dake Bible, page 427 says:

"The doctrine of the remnant of men saved always refers to Judah and the other tribes of Israel, never to Gentiles or the Church. It expresses the idea that God is under obligation to all Israel to save a remnant of them, so as to preserve their seed to fulfill with them eventually, the Covenants made with Abraham, Isaac, Jacob, and David to whom He promised an eternal seed and to the seed an eternal land. (Genesis 12:1-3, 7; 13:14-17; 15:18-21; 17:2-8,19; 21:12; 22:17-18; 26:3-4; 28: 3-4, 13-15; 2 Samuel 7).

Many times God predicted the deliverance and preservation of a remnant of the 12 tribes and their final and eternal restoration under their Messiah, (Isaiah 1:9, 10: 20-22; 11:10-12, 16; 38:31-32; 46:3; Jeremiah 23:3; 31:7, 39:9; 40:11; Ezekiel 6:8-10, Joel 2:32; Micah 2:12, 5:3-8; Zephaniah 2: 7-9; 3:13; Zechariah 8:6-12; Romans 9:27;11:5; Revelation 12:17). According to Isaiah 1:9, a prediction was made that a very small remnant would be saved in the coming destruction of Judah and Jerusalem; otherwise, Israel would have been totally destroyed like Sodom and Gomorrah."

Jewish Apostasy (Isaiah 1:10; Deuteronomy 32:32)

There is a connection between Jewish apostasy and the Jewish remnant. The apostasy of Israel can be framed in all the times the nation fell flat on its face before God. God would proclaim Himself to the Israelites; they would delight in that and there would be a period of peace. Then the Israelites would forget about God, turn to Baal worship, and continually worship idols of surrounding heathen nations. The anger of God would come to the surface and He would send enemies against them, be they Syrians, Philistines, or whoever. The Israelites would realize their helpless state, cry out to God and repent of their apostasy and be bailed out by God. This would repeat over and over again until the Diaspora, after which we now find Israel back in their nation once again. However, they are in an apostate condition again, being blinded to their Messiah, the Lord Jesus Christ.

> *"For I would not, brethren, that ye should be ignorant of this mystery lest ye should be wise in your own conceits; that blindness in part is happened to Israel, until the fulness of the Gentiles be come in."* (Romans 11:25)

The ending of the unbelief in Israel and the fullness of the Gentiles are future events and the former is dependent on the latter. As of now, the blindness of unbelief envelops Israel along with liberalism and their apostasy. They can expect to be cut off soon and cannot be saved until end time events are played out.

So what are the reasons that Israel has fallen so many times as recorded in the Old Testament, and suffered the Diaspora, only to be given back the land temporarily, and are now on the verge of having it taken away from them again? Israel will again be held accountable and their future will again hinge upon a faithful remnant for their continuance. Why?

We find reasons for Israel's falling as a nation in the book of Hosea.[2] There was a famine in the land for God's words. The words and their meanings were not getting into the hearts of the people and were nearly sealed off to the children. It is a far cry from the days of the Scripture readings by Ezra and the Levites to the people. "So they read in the book in the Law of God distinctly, and gave the sense, and caused them to understand the reading. (Nehemiah 8:8). Because there is no knowledge of God and His words, it leads to a total rejection of His knowledge. This degeneration causes swearing, lying, killing and stealing, as well as adultery and bloody violence. They lost their priesthood and all spiritual contact with their God. Idolatry increased along with the worship of idols.

The recurrent theme of Jewish apostasy shows up again and again throughout the book of Judges. Judges 2:11; "And the children of Israel did evil in the sight of the Lord, and served Baalim." This is the result of the lack of knowledge of God in the land and in their hearts. It will follow that idol worship will return, God turns His back on them, they are enslaved, then they cry out of deliverance.

> "And they forsook the Lord God of their fathers, which brought them out of the Land of Egypt, and followed other gods, of the gods of the people that were round about them, and bowed themselves unto them, and provoked the Lord to anger." (Judges 2:12)

They leave the high station of the worship of God and openly commit spiritual adultery as they enter the second phase of their apostasy. They get to the point of severe foolishness by inquiring of dead idols for their counsel.

> "My people ask counsel at their stocks, " (Hosea 4:12)

> "...shall I fall down to the stock of a tree?" (Isaiah 44:19)

> "Saying to a stock, thou art my father; and to a stone, thou hast brought me forth:" (Jeremiah 2:27)

This is the lowest of the forms of worship for the Israelites. It has degraded to a worship of trees and stones, and the utter contempt of calling them their father when they had rejected the Father in Heaven who had begotten them.

This leads to the next phase of apostasy where pride has risen in their hearts, sin has prevailed and pride goeth before their destruction.

> *"And the pride of Israel doth testify to his face; therefore shall Israel and Ephraim fall in their inequity; Judah also shall fall with them."*
> (Hosea 5:5)

What did Israel have to be so full of pride about? Why were they so puffed up with themselves?

Hosea 5.5 states:

> *"And the pride of Israel doth testify to his face; therefore shall Israel and Ephraim fall in their inequity; Judah also shall fall with them."*

All of Israel eventually turned their backs to God, and did not even consider returning to Him or seeking Him. Pride caused Israel to not obey God and it set Israel up for destruction. "Pride goeth before destruction, and an haughty spirit before a fall." So we see pride bringing in apostasy and operating within its confines.

Another factor leading to apostasy is instability of character or double mindedness. Failing to learn more knowledge of God for spiritual growth, committing spiritual adultery, and being full of pride will contribute to instability in God's people where they need to be always strong and firm in the Lord. There will be no goodness, kindness, or mercy in God's people since they have blocked God's goodness, kindness, and mercy from working through them.

Because of all this confusion, God's people will offer to God things that he does not desire and cannot use. This disobedience is sin and treachery to the Almighty. It will lead to a mixing with the world.

> *"Ephraim, he hath mixed himself among the people; Ephraim is a cake, not turned."* (Hosea 7:8).

> *"Love not the world, neither the things that are in the world."* (1 John 2:15)

Corruption and deep apostasy will take over a nation and a people as an immoral soul is entrenched. This will, over time, in combination with all the other gradual stages, stir God to move on excessive sin. This sinning will seem to go on for a long time, but God takes notice.

> *"They have deeply corrupted themselves, as in the days of Gibeah: therefore, he will remember their inequity, he will visit their sins.* (Hosea 9:9).

In the final stages of apostasy the Church will be worldly and true believers will be shunned as strange.

> *"For the time will come when they will not endure sound doctrine; but after their own lusts shall they heap to themselves teachers, having itching ears; and they shall turn away their ears from the truth, and shall be turned unto fables.* (2 Timothy 4:3-4)

"For it had been better for them not to have known the way of righteousness, then, after they have known it, to turn from the holy commandment delivered unto them. (2 Peter 2:21)

Times of the Gentiles

Finally, it has to happen.

"And they shall fall by the edge of the sword, and shall be led away captive into all nations: and Jerusalem shall be trodden down of the Gentiles, until the times of the Gentiles be fulfilled." Luke 21:24

Israel was so deep in its apostasy that God acted. The Ten Tribes of Israel and then Judah gave up on God, and God gave up on them. The same was true of the Jews in 70 A.D.

"And even as they did not like to retain God in their knowledge, God gave them over to a reprobate mind, to do those things which are not convenient:' (Romans 1:28)

Thus, filled with all unrighteousness they are actively doing all the works of the flesh, (Romans 1:29-31). There is an understanding that these things are worthy of death and yet they do them anyway. The times of the Gentiles begin with Nebuchadnezzar's conquest of Judah . It is roughly 605 B.C. that the first wave of Israelites are taken into captivity, Daniel included. Jerusalem is thus introduced to the trodding down of the Gentiles between the Babylonian captivity until the end of the Tribulation period and the glorious coming of our Lord Jesus Christ.

It is significant to realize that in our present day we are still in the time of the Gentiles. When

Christ is crucified and cut off the sixty-ninth week of Daniel's prophecy ends. The prophetic clock of Israel stopped for Israel, and will not resume until the Tribulation begins. This happens when the Antichrist signs a covenant with Israel for 1 week (7 years) and Israel's prophetic clock starts again.

> "And he shall confirm the covenant with many for one week: and in the midst of the week he shall cause the sacrifice and the oblation to cease,." (Daniel 9:27).

There is a great space of time during the 69th week of Daniel, after 33 A.D. roughly, and the seventieth week of Daniel, which will be fulfilled after the Church is raptured. The Church age began at Pentecost (yes, Pentecost) and will end with the meeting with Christ in the air at the Rapture.

> "Then we which are alive and remain shall be caught up together with them (the dead in Christ) in the clouds, to meet the Lord in the air:" (1 Thessalonians 4:17)

At that time (Pentecost), saw the coming of the Holy Spirit and He created the Church by baptizing believers into the body of Christ.

> "For by one spirit are we all baptized into one body, whether we be Jews or Gentiles, whether we be bond or free; and have been all made to drink into one spirit.": (1 Corinthians 12:13)

> "Where there is neither Greek nor Jew, circumcision nor uncircumcision,…bond or free; but Christ is all, and in all." (Colossians 3:11)

The Church age is running its course within the times of the Gentiles, up to the Rapture. This present church age was not seen in the Old Testament. At the close of the church age there will be seen:

> *"Knowing this first, that there shall come in the last days scoffers, walking after their own lusts, and saying, Where is the promise of his coming?"* (2 Peter 3:3-4)

After the Rapture of the Church, the Antichrist will arise and will then antagonize the Tribulation saints and also directly with the nation of Israel along with the rest of the Gentile nations. He will form his global government, the Beast, and Israel will be able to rebuild the Temple and a resurgence of pre-exilic sacrifices and offerings will be re-established.

The new Jewish resurgent religious community along with the global apostate church will help out the Antichrist with his worldwide global ambitions. The apostate, fallen church, is the institutional worldly church that is present on earth after the true Christian church, the true body of Christ, is snatched up by Christ at the Rapture.

The Jews are still in Jerusalem midway through the Tribulation, and have their temple, but are under Gentile rule,

> *"But the court which is without the temple leave out, and measure it not; for it is given unto the Gentiles; and the holy city shall they tread under foot forty and two months."* (Revelation 11:2)

The apostate church will be destroyed right at the mid tribulation point. After that will come intense persecution by the Antichrist of the Jewish nation because many of the Jews will refuse to worship and Antichrist as their Messiah. Two-thirds of the Jewish population in Israel will be destroyed, one-third will be shepherded to safety as the holy remnant and preserved, and the Antichrist and his armies will be destroyed by Christ at the battle of Armageddon."

> *"And the beast was taken, and with him the false prophet that wrought miracles before him, with which he deceived them that had received the mark of the beast, and them that worshipped his image, these both were cast alive into a lake of fire burning with brimstone."* (Revelation 19:20)

With the destruction of the Antichrist and his minions by a triumphant Christ Jesus, the times of the Gentiles come to an end.

Literal Interpretation of Prophecy

We have seen that the great apostasy of Israel led to the captivity first of the Ten Tribes of Israel and then the Babylonian Captivity of Judah. The treading down of the city of Jerusalem by the Gentiles triggered the beginning of the times of the Gentiles and the rise of the Gentile empires which paved the way for the gospel to go out to the Gentiles and end times prophecies to come through the prophet Daniel.

Since we will be discussing empires and prophecy, a clear understanding of how Scripture as it applies to prophecy needs to be interpreted.

Many years ago David L. Cooper set out what he called the Golden Rule of Interpretation: "When the plain sense of Scripture makes common sense, seek no other sense: therefore, take every word at its primary, ordinary, usual, literal, meaning unless the facts of the immediate context, studied in the light of related passages and axiomatic and fundamental truth, indicate clearly otherwise."[3]

Unless otherwise indicated, this book and its author take the position that the Bible is best interpreted and understood literally and dispensationally.

> *"And I said unto the angel that talked with me, what be these? And he answered me, these are the horns which have scattered Juda, Israel, and Jerusalem.* (Zechariah 1:19)

The Gentile Empires – Nebuchadnezzar's Dream

We have just left the explanation of the times of the Gentiles. The word Gentile designates all the non-Jewish people and nations of the world. This is the period in time that is God's program of rule and salvation for the Gentile nations.

Daniel was to interpret the prophetic dream God had given the Babylonian King, thus saving a multitude of magicians, astrologers, sorcerers, and the Chaldeans from being slain. The decree had already gone forth that the wise men should be slain along with Daniel and his fellows. God brought the dream to Daniel's understanding for the sake of all the people living then even up to today for God's understanding of the history of the world to be understood.

The dream is given in Daniel 2:31-33:

> *"Thou, O King, sawest, and behold a great image. This great mage, whose brightness was*

excellent, stood before thee; and the form thereof was terrible.

This image's head was of fine gold, his breast and his arms of silver, his belly and his thighs of brass,

His legs of iron, his feet part of iron and part of clay."

The interpretation of the dream and the image is given to us in Daniel 2:38-43. The King of Babylon was the head of gold. God had given Nebuchadnezzar total authority over all the peoples, beasts of the field and fowls of the air. Nothing could happen unless the king authorized it.

Another kingdom would supplant Babylon which would be the Medo-Persian Empire. After that would come the Grecian Empire with Alexander the Great at its head.

The fourth empire has come and run its course in history but has split into two main parts, lying dormant, but already refueling the revived Roman Empire. This was prophesied in Daniel 2:40;

"...forasmuch as iron breaketh in pieces and subdueth all things; and as iron that breaketh all these, shall it break in pieces and bruise."

Thus, the two legs of iron are fulfilled in the eastern and western Roman empires. The pieces that it has broken into are represented by the nation once in the empire. The Roman form of government is preserved in the eastern leg as Germany and in the western leg today in Russia. Rome would be revived through an organized European Union through which a world leader will emerge.

Daniel 2:42-43 says,

"and as the toes of the feet were part of iron, and part of clay, so the kingdom shall be partly strong, and partly broken.. 43 And whereas thou sawest iron mixed with miry clay, they shall mingle themselves with the seed of men; but they shall not cleave one to another, even as iron is not mixed with clay."

These pieces, or nations which have been broken apart, will never adhere together as one but continually split from each other and loosely form a kingdom at the end of the age. Today this is known as the European Union from which is yet to emerge the one world leader known as Antichrist. Man's day, the Times of the Gentiles, in the form of world empires will end and the Lord's day will reign.

The Babylonian Empire first removed the Jews from the land. This first primary remnant of Jews returned to rebuild Jerusalem and the temple led by Ezra and Nehemiah. It was the Roman empire that caused the Diaspora, the scattering of the Jews, starting in 70 AD.

The prophetic part of Nebuchadnezzar's dream is yet to be fulfilled. Christ will come and set up an everlasting kingdom which will break all the other kingdoms into pieces and consume them.

Daniel 2:45 says:

"Forasmuch as thou sawest that the stone was cut out of the mountain without hands, and that it brake in pieces the iron, the brass, the clay, the silver, and the gold;"

That stone is the Lord Jesus Christ and He is yet to come to bring a close to the times of the Gentiles.

Seventy Weeks of Daniel – Daniel 9:24-27

Jerusalem is God's time clock for the end times and it is now in the hands of the Jews and we are still living in "the Times of the Gentiles." There will rise a world leader who will wrest control of the holy city away from them and that this wicked ruler will severely persecute God's people – the Jews. This last evil ruler is mentioned in Daniel 9:24-27.

> *"Seventy weeks are determined upon thy people and upon thy holy city, to finish the transgression, and to make an end of sins, and to make reconciliation for iniquity, and to bring in everlasting righteousness, and to seal up the vision and prophecy, and to anoint the most holy.*
>
> *25 Know therefore and understand, that from the going forth of the commandment to restore and to build Jerusalem unto the Messiah the Prince shall be seven weeks, and threescore and two weeks: the street shall be built again, and the wall, even in troublous times.*
>
> *26 And after threescore and two weeks shall Messiah be cut off, but not for himself: and the people of the prince that shall come shall destroy the city and the sanctuary; and the end there of shall be with a flood, and unto the end of the war desolations are determined.*
>
> *27 And he shall confirm the covenant with many for one week: and in the midst of the week he shall cause the sacrifice and the oblation to cease, and for the overspreading of abomination he shall make it desolate, even until the*

consummation, and that determined shall be poured upon the desolate."

The prophecy in Daniel 9 tells us that the horn of David, Jesus Christ the King of Israel, would be cut off from His people until the abomination of the little horn, the Antichrist, is disposed of.

"And through his (Antichrist's) policy also he shall cause craft to prosper in his hand; and he shall magnify himself in his heart and by peace shall destroy many: he shall also stand up against the Prince of princes; but he shall be broken without hand" (Daniel 8:25)

This prophecy given to Daniel has everything to do with Daniel's people and Daniel's city which would be the nation of Israel and the city of Jerusalem. Daniel was deported and in Babylonian captivity and was reading Jeremiah when he understood that the seventy years of servitude were nearly concluded. Therefore, he prayed for his people, the Israelites; that their bondage would end and they would be delivered.

They were being punished:

"And this whole land shall be a desolation, and an astonishment; and these nations shall serve the king of Babylon seventy years" (Jeremiah 25:11)

Now was the time for Israel's return.

"For thus saith the Lord, that after seventy years be accomplished at Babylon I will visit you, and perform my good work toward you, in causing you to return to this place." (Jeremiah 29:10).

Thus, we have the prophecy given to Daniel who would then make his people understand: From

Daniel 9:24 to Daniel 9:27, Verse 24 would be the outline of the entire prophecy; Verse 25 would explain 69 weeks; Verse 26 we find the gap of time between week 69 and 70; and Verse 27 we have the 70th week of Daniel.

Daniel's prophecy covered 70 weeks, or 70 weeks of 7 years, or 490 years. This is in accordance with the Hebrew accounting of time. This is first taught to us in Numbers 14:34.

> *"After the number of the days in which ye searched the land, even forty days, each day for a year, shall ye bear your iniquities, even forty years, and ye shall know my breach of promise."*

> *"I have appointed thee each day for a year."* (Ezekiel 4:66)

God told Israel to send spies to search out the land before the Israelites were to first occupy it. They took forty days and reported back with faithless forecasts of doom and defeat if they dared to attempt taking the land. So, God responded to their lack of faith by making them wander for forty years in the desert, one year for each day.

Thus, we are to look beyond the casual and superficial view of the word week, meaning only one thing, a period of seven days. Rather, seventy weeks must proceed to be translated from days into years. God makes known unto Daniel that by the space of the seventy weeks, or sevens of years, the total of prophecies in regards to His people Israel will be fulfilled.

The beginning of this seventy week prophecy has a definite fixed point; "from the going forth of the Commandment to restore and to build Jerusalem." (V 25). There is not total agreement with Scripture as to which of the commandments (decrees) and their date would and should be used as the starting point. There were four decrees issued by Persian and Median kings that had something to do with the rebuilding of Jerusalem and the rebuilding of the Temple.

The first decree was written by Cyrus king of Persia in 536 B.C. This fulfilled Jeremiah's prophecy that the Jews would start to return to the land after seventy years of captivity in Babylon. It is mentioned in Ezra 1:1-4 and was about the rebuilding of the house of God which is the Temple. The 490 year prophecy could not begin without a decree given to rebuild Jerusalem, the city.

The second decree was given by Darius the Mede, the year, 519 B.C. Ezra 5:1-17 related the story that the building of the Temple was impeded by those who claimed there was no proper authority for such a project. Darius then searched the Treasure house in which was found the original parchment of the first decree of Cyrus, seventeen years previous. Darius then wrote a reaffirmation of the decree of Cyrus, thus it concerned only the rebuilding of the Temple.

In the third decree, that of Artaxerxes the king of Persia, was a letter taken by Ezra to Jerusalem. Written in 458 B.C. permission was given for the priests and Levites who were willing to return to Israel. It reinstated Temple services, authorized the collection of gold and silver to purchase animals for sacrifice, and also made available Persian Treasury funds for the project. What the money could buy and how much was available is found in Ezra7:11-22. Nothing was contained in this third decree about restoring or rebuilding Jerusalem. It was a letter for a faithful and determined Ezra who wished to see that the law was carried out for the service in the house of the Lord.

The all important fourth decree was that of Artaxerxes Longimanus, given in 445 B.C. It was recorded in Nehemiah 2:1-8. It started when Artaxerxes noticed Nehemiah's sad expression on his face. Being the king's cup-bearer, the king would necessarily be very concerned if his food and wine taster became ill. Nehemiah assured the king that the food was not poisoned and that the reason for his sadness was found in Nehemiah 2:3; "Why should not my countenance be sad, when the city, the place of my father's sepulchers, lieth waste, and the gates thereof are consumed with fire?"

Nehemiah was given a letter by Artaxerxes for the keeper of the king's forest for timber to build the wall around Jerusalem and other parts of the city. Fifty-two days were required to repair the walls and twelve years were needed to rebuild and restore the city and re-establish the law to fulfill the prophecy.

> *"And it came to pass in the month Hisan,*
> *in the twentieth year of Artaxerxes the king..."*
> (Nehemiah 2:1)

Even the Encyclopedia Britannica, certainly not biased in favor of prophecy, sets the date of Artaxerxes' accession as 465 B.C.; and therefore his twentieth year would be 445 B.C.; the month was Nisan, and, since no day is given, according to Jewish custom the date would be understood as the first. Hence in our calendar the date would be

March 14, 445 B.C. Here we have the beginning of the seventy weeks.[4]

This then is the beginning date of God's call to the Jewish remnant to gather and return to Israel, and more precisely Jerusalem. From their going forth from March 14, 445 B.C. to restore and to rebuild Jerusalem unto the coming of the Messiah, the Lord Jesus Christ, would be seven weeks, and sixty two weeks. Nehemiah had the workforce be clad in their armor and work with one hand and hold a weapon in the other. Such was the troublous times that harassed them. Fort-nine years, seven weeks, it took to repair the city and the wall, completed in 396 B.C.

From the completion of the rebuilding of Jerusalem until the coming of the Messiah would be sixty-two weeks, or 434 years. The total number of years of rebuilding Jerusalem to the coming of the Messiah would be 483 years. The Verse (5) of Chapter 9 does not specify whether the conception, birth, baptism, crucifixion, or resurrection of the Lord Jesus Christ is meant.[5]

"And after threescore and two weeks..."

The key here in Verse 26 is that after the rebuilding of Jerusalem and 62 weeks shall the Lord Jesus Christ, the Messiah, be cut off. This is after the end of the sixty-ninth week. During this time after the conclusion of the sixty-ninth week two things were to happen. First, the Messiah was to be cut off. Second, the city of Jerusalem and the Temple were to be destroyed.

"Cut off" means to die. Isaiah 53:8 says, "...for he was cut off out of the land of the living: for the transgression of my people was he stricken." The Lord Jesus Christ was cut off for the sins of the people at the Crucifixion. Two days before Christ was to be crucified he gave His Olivet Discourse and He was already past the triumphal entry into Jerusalem and past the 69th week. Some say that the first part of the 70th week was the 33-1/2 years of the life of Christ and the rest of the 70th week is the nearly 2000 years we are in now, known as the Age of Grace. This is a fallacy since the 70th week cannot be stretched out any longer than 7 years.

So what we have in Daniel 9:26 is plainly an interval between the 69th and 70th week.

The Gap

In Verse 26 we have no mention of the completion of the 490 years from the cutting off of the Messiah to the destruction of the Temple or the final ending of the 70th week. When Christ was not enthroned upon the throne of David, and He was killed, God stopped the prophetic clock. The sins and iniquity of Israel caused the breach of God's promise between the 69th week and the 70th week of the prophecy. Prophetic has stopped at the end of the 69th week and the 70th week has not started, therefore, one week has yet to be fulfilled. This period of time from the end of the 69th week to the beginning of the 70th week is called a "gap." This distinct interval is known as the dispensation of Grace. This is what God addresses as a breach of His promise to Israel:

> *"After the number of the days in which ye searched the land, even forty days, each day for a year, shall ye bear your iniquities, even forty*

years, and ye shall know my breach of promise."
(Numbers 14:34)

God has breached his promise because of the iniquity and transgressions of Israel which caused God to stop prophetic time between the 69th and 70th in which is now a time-gap. But God will not allow His breach of promise to cancel His promises to Israel nor deter the Almighty from doing what He said He would do.

> "*Moreover the light of the moon shall be as the light of the sun, and the light of the sun shall be seven fold, as the light of seven days, in the day that the Lord bindeth up the breach of his people, and healeth the stroke of their wound.*"
> (Isiah 30:26)

Right after the Triumphal entry of Christ into Jerusalem, He stood on the Mount of Olives and gave His Olivet Discourse. The 69 weeks were behind Him and He was two days out from the "after threescore and two weeks..." (V26) when Christ was to be cut off. In the Olivet Discourse Christ Jesus prophesied that Jerusalem was going to be destroyed and be trodden down until the fulfillment of the Times of the Gentiles. Jesus Christ will return in the clouds for His church at the Rapture. This is the all-inclusive gap of more than 1980 years and ends the dispensation and Age of Grace, between the 69th and 70th week. The "Olivet Discourse" is the key to the interpretation of Daniel 9: 26-27.

A third thing about Verse 26 is that a prince would come that is not Messiah the Prince, and he would be of his people that would destroy Jerusalem. We know that the Romans under

General Vespasian sent his son, Captain Titus, then named General by his father, was in charge of the siege. When Vespasian became emperor, Titus was made a prince. His army lost its mind and became uncontrolled as recorded by Josephus and the people of the prince destroyed the city and the sanctuary, just as it says in Verse 26.

> *"And the end thereof shall be with a flood, and unto the end of the war desolations are determined."* (Daniel 9:26b)

There will be war and desolations all the way until the end when the Lord Jesus Christ will return with the armies of heaven and destroy the armies of the Antichrist who had gathered to prevent the second coming of Israel's Messiah. At the time of Christ's victory He will fulfill God's promise to Israel stated in Verse 24 as to the reasons for the seventy weeks prophecy.

The promise was to:
1. To finish the transgression.
2. To make an end of sins.
3. To make reconciliation for iniquity.
4. To bring in everlasting righteousness.
5. To seal up the vision and prophecy.
6. To anoint the most holy.

Keep in mind that these promises pertain only to the Jews and Jerusalem and that they have nothing to do with Gentiles or Christians that make up the church. Finishing the transgression means the putting away of transgressions of the law and commandments by Israel, the Jews. The Transgression is not yet finished, and will not be brought to an end until Christ returns to rule on the throne of David and Israel repents and turns to God.

To make an end to sin means that Israel, as a nation, shall turn away from their sins and accept the Lord Jesus Christ as their Saviour. "This is my covenant unto them, when I take away their sins." (Romans 11:27). Although the Jews are back in Israel temporarily, if a Jew would die in his sin, he or she goes to hell just the same as a Gentile. When Jesus appears at the end of the Tribulation they will then be saved from their sins when they know it is their Messiah standing in front of them.

Making reconciliation for iniquity means that the wickedness that surrounds the sinful condition of Israel will lead to the recognition of their Messiah at His second coming. When He appears to Israel the nation in all His glory, they will look upon Him when they have pierced, and the nation shall be converted in a day.

> *"Who hath heard such a thing? Who hath seen such things? Shall the earth be made to bring forth in one day? Or shall a nation be born at once? For as soon as Zion Travailed, she brought forth her children."* (Isaiah 66:8).

To bring in everlasting Righteousness will not happen until Christ Jesus comes to prevail over all Israel when the millennial kingdom is set up. As sinful human beings we have no righteousness of our own. Man attains imputed righteousness through faith in Jesus Christ, and this will happen for Israel when the receive Christ Jesus as their Messiah.

"Israel shall dwell safely: and this is his name whereby he shall be called, THE LORD OUR RIGHTEOUSNESS." (Jeremiah 23:6)

To seal up the vision and prophecy does not necessarily mean the vision and prophecy given here to Daniel. All of the prophesies that are recorded in the Bible were given to Israelites, and all prophecy is sealed up in Israel. To seal is from the Hebrew *"Chatham,"* meaning to set a seal upon, seal up as is Israel's testimony or law is sealed or imprinted upon the Jews for future reference.

"Bind up the testimony, seal the law among my disciples." (Isaiah 8:16)

The visions and the prophecies have been sealed and limited to the Jewish race and when they began to return back to their land did the understanding of these prophesies apply to the last days.

To anoint the Most Holy is the last mentioned promise to Daniel and Israel means the sanctification of the Temple with the Messiah present therein. This happens when Jesus Christ enters his Millennial Temple. There will be a new Temple, the Millennial Temple, built right after the Rapture of the Church, during the very early part of the Tribulation. The glory of the Lord filled the Wilderness Tabernacle and was present in the Holy of Holies.

*"Then a cloud covered the tent of the Congregation, and the glory of the Lord filled the tabernacle." (*Exodus 40:34)

37

Ezekiel 41 and 42 has within them the prophet's vision of the end time Temple and Ezekiel 43 has the return of glory to it to anoint the Most Holy.

> *"Afterward he brought me to the gate, even the gate that looketh toward the east: And, behold, the glory of the God of Israel came from the way of the east:"* (Ezekiel 43:1,2a.)

> *"And the glory of the Lord of the Lord came into the house by the way of the gate whose prospect is toward the east."* (Ezekiel 43:4)

These six things that Daniel had prayed for Israel will be fulfilled when the nation of Israel looks upon the Risen Lord and knows Him as Messiah. The Messiah came to Israel at the end of the 69 prophetic weeks only to be cut off. At the last day of the 70th week the Messiah would fulfill all six things promised to Daniel. The six part promise gives us the purpose of the Seventy Weeks Prophecy without which there would be no reason for the Prophecy at all or God's promise to Israel.

> *"And being fully persuaded that, what he had promised, he was able also to perform."* (Romans 4:21)

Olive Tree

An examination of the olive tree in Scripture and who Israel really is, is now in order. The three types of trees or rooted structures that are used to symbolize Israel in the Bible are the "vine", the "fig" tree and the "olive" tree. The fig tree and the vine, according to Clarence Larkin, prefigure the Millennial days, Micah 4:4 says:

> *"But they shall sit every man under his*
> *vine and under his fig tree; and none shall make*
> *them afraid: for the mouth of the Lord of hosts*
> *hath spoken it."*

The "Vine" is a symbol of Israel's Spiritual privileges.

The "Fig-tree" is a symbol of Israel' National privileges.[6]

Although a symbol for millennial blessing, a rebellious Israel is referred to as "wild grapes," an "empty vine,", "The degenerate plant of a strange vine" (Isa.5:2, 4; Jer. 2:21; Hosea 10:1)[7]

The Vine symbolizes the spiritual bond between Himself and His people who were brought out from Egypt to be transplanted in the promised Canaan. It was planted in righteousness from an un-regenerated plant and when needed to bring forth good grapes God found something different.

> *"Yet I had planted thee a noble vine,*
> *wholly a right seed: how then art thou turned into*
> *the degenerate plant of a strange vine unto me?:"*
> (Jeremiah 2:21.)

Because Israel took the Heir to the vineyard (Jesus) and cast Him out and cut Him off it has been turned over to the Gentiles.

> *"And they caught him, and case him out of*
> *the vineyard, and slew him.*
>
> *...and will let out his vineyard unto other*
> *husbandmen, which shall render him the fruits in*
> *their seasons"* (Matthew 21:39-41b)

With the use of the olive tree by Paul, God's sovereign plan for Israel and the Gentiles is revealed. Israel's place in God's plan in its past, present, and future and the Gentiles place in God's plan are revealed to us.

> *"Serve the Lord with fear, and rejoice with trembling." "Kiss the son, lest he be angry, and ye perish from the way, when his wrath is kindled but a little. Blessed are all they that put their trust in him."* (Psalm 2:11, 12)

The blessing for the Gentiles was dependent upon Israel's obedience to God. Peter preached the Jews rejection of their Messiah:

> *"Him, being delivered by the determinate counsel and foreknowledge of God, ye have taken, and by wicked hands have crucified and slain:"* (Acts 2:23)

God had raised up Paul the Apostle and delivered to him a new plan of blessing and salvation through the gospel for Gentiles. God would pour out His mercy and would use Paul as the Apostle to the Gentiles (Romans 11:13).

> *"Testifying both to the Jews, and also to the Greeks, repentance toward God, and faith toward our Lord Jesus Christ."* (Acts 20:21).

> *"For I delivered unto you first of all that which I also received, not that Christ died for our sins according to the scriptures; and that he was buried, and that he rose again the third day according to the scriptures:"* (1 Corinthians 15: 3-4)

Paul presents a mystery and this mystery is symbolized by the olive tree in Romans 11.

> *"For I would not, brethren, that ye should be ignorant of this mystery, lest ye should be wise in your own conceits; that blindness in part is*

happened to Israel, until the fulness of the Gentiles be come in.": (Romans II:25).

The biblical symbolism starts with a root, in Romans 11:16:

"For if the first fruit be holy, the lump is also holy; and if the root be holy, so are the branches."

Paul has set about proving that Israel's history of rejection and hardness has not resulted in God's permanently setting them aside. Israel had the Messiah in their vision and midst and could not recognize Him they were so blind. This blindness and disobedience had been going on a very long time.

Israel had always been seeking after righteousness but had always failed due to going about it through their works. Their hearts were hardened; in the Greek, *"poroo,"* meaning to be hardened, make hard like a stone and to be callous, insensitive.

"Yet the Lord hath not given you a heart to perceive, and eyes to see, and ears to hear, unto this day." (Deuteronomy 29:4)

This blindness and hardness exists today and Israel in their land is not saved. But this condition will one day in the future be lifted.

"And they shall look upon me whom they have pierced and they shall mourn for him," (Zechariah 12:10b)

David is quoted in Romans 11:9 from the great suffering Psalm 69:22: "Let their table become a snare before them: and that which should have been for their welfare, let it become a trap." The table refers to the Passover which looked forward to Calvary and their Messiah. Jesus Christ was the Passover Lamb who was looked for since that first Passover in Egypt. But Israel was blinded by darkened eyes as the Lord Jesus hung on the cross. The fear of that first Passover night as the killing angel went forth is still upon Israel. The table of Israel, the Passover has become a snare to Israel until today. By continuing to observe Passover year after year, it is a snare and a trap to them since they keep looking forward for the Messiah. The blessing that was meant for the Jews, them finding their Messiah and their salvation, has become a curse.

In Romans 11:14 we have an interesting verse, where Paul is pouring out his heart for the fulfillment of God's purpose for Israel.

> *"If by any means I may provoke to emulation them which are my flesh, and might save some of them."*

Improbable as it seemed even to Paul, it (Israel's blindness) did not deter Paul in his mission for God. He coveted Gentile and Jewish converts to Jesus. He followed the plan to provoke his fellow Israelites according to the flesh to follow the Gentiles to be saved. For Paul it made no difference who would be saved, just so he might save some Jews. Paul strove to stir up the Jews by the spiritual blessings bestowed upon the Gentiles to motivate Jews to be saved. The Jews then and now spend much time and energy doing good works which get them nowhere with God. In their frustration, we Christians must inspire Jews to emulate us to salvation by being spiritually attractive to them.

Brush aside those who would discourage giving Jews the gospel, and then pronounce the coming judgments upon them. This is anti-Semitism in its worst form. When Jews see peace, joy, faith, satisfaction and contentment in Jesus, purpose, and love in us, they will be moved to jealousy and be open to Jesus Christ.

> *"For if the casting away of them be the reconciling of the world, what shall the receiving of them be, but life from the dead?"*

This is where Paul is leaving no doubt but that God is not permanently through with Israel yet and never intended to be. The purpose of God in setting aside Israel temporarily was for the gospel to go forth for the benefit of the world and for Christ to build His church. This is crucial for Christians to understand. God is calling out Gentiles and Jews with the gospel in order to build His church. This is crucial for Christians to understand. Anything else that is mixed into that is supersessionism and antisemitism. The Israelites were given the gospel, they did not believe and God had to move them aside so that the Gentiles could hear the Good News and be added to the church.

Paul, in Verse 15 is looking forward to the time that Israel will be saved and the rest of the world will be blessed during the millennial kingdom. "...what shall the receiving of them be, but life from the dead?" Paul invites all to look forward to the time that Israel will be reborn, regenerated, and will be the head and not the tail, but the leader of all nations.

"And the Lord shall make thee the head, and not the tail; and thou shalt be above only, and thou shalt not be beneath;" (Deuteronomy 28:13)

Paul now turns to the Olive Tree as the illustration of Christ's mercy and salvation.

"...and if the root be holy, so are the branches. And if some of the branches be broken off, and thou, being a wild olive tree, wert grafted in among them, and with them partakest of the root and fatness of the olive tree;" (Romans 11:16b, 17)

The Olive Tree, as do all trees, begins with a root, together with its branches. This root we know to be Christ and He is holy, the symbol for the one holy and eternal creator God. This root is the beginning in creation of everything that is holy and growing in holiness from one spiritual root. Christ is that root as is stated in John 1:1:

"In the beginning was the Word, and the Word was with God, and the Word was God."

If the root of the tree was Christ, and He was consecrated and holy unto God, then the branches (Israel) are also set apart unto Him. This was true as long as the atoning sacrifices were still acceptable to God.

The olive tree symbolically represents God's restoration of the rejected nation of Israel back to her place of privilege. The host and olive tree, which is Christ symbolically, shows that the holy branches were in a place of blessing which stemmed from the unconditional covenant God made with Abraham. The branches represent the Jewish people.

Paul says in Verse 17 that unsaved Jews, the branches of national Israel, have been broken off temporarily. Therefore, some of the branches had fallen and had to be cut off.

> *"I say then, have they stumbled that they should fall? God forbid: but rather through their fall salvation is come unto the Gentiles, for to provoke them to jealousy* (Romans 11:1)

God took this opportunity to graft in other branches from a wild olive tree to be in the root and fatness of the olive tree. These, of course, are the same Gentiles from the time of the start of the Great Commission until now. This term, wild olive tree, *"agrielaios,"* is only found in this verse (17) and in verse 24. The word, thou, in this Verse (17) links it to the saved Gentiles to whom Paul was speaking. These two groups of believers are both partaking of the spiritual blessings that come from the Covenant of Abraham.

Spiritual pride on the part of believers must not be lifted up against unbelieving Jews. This leads to the belief that Jews have been cast off for good and that the Church is the replacement for Israel with all of its promises being appropriated.

Israel, in the form of the olive tree's branches, was broken off for the sole reason of unbelief in the Lord Jesus Christ as the Messiah, as stated in Verse 20. Christians in Paul's time had developed a superior attitude towards the Jews and Paul reminded them that they stood before Christ by faith. Christians are to guard against ever being high-minded. The Greek word for high-minded is,*"hupselophroneo."* This is to be proud or arrogant. It is thinking that one is great, or somebody to be reckoned with.

The Scripture says that God loved the people of Israel as His chosen people. However, God did not spare the natural branches, (Israel) after so much time of them rejecting Him, and He could no longer spare even His chosen. God will cut off those who reject His Son, just like He had done to Israel. "Why should God have any more regard for a faithless Gentile Christianity, than for a faithless Judaism? [8] The fact exists with God that the false Gentile church can be cut off for unbelief, as it is also possible for Israel to be grafted back in for believing the Gospel.

> "And they also, if they abide not still in unbelief, shall be graffed in. For God is able to graff them in again. For if thou wert cut out of the olive tree which is wild by nature, and went graffed contrary to nature into a good olive tree: how much more shall these, which be the natural branches, be graffed into their own olive tree?" (Romans 11: 23-24)

God is holding out to Israel the possibility through His infinite mercy, to receive Christ in the future. He offers the promise that Israel would be graffed back into the olive tree once again. If Israel ever wants what was given to the Gentiles, then God in willing, able, and waiting to return them to their rightful place.

That word graff, graffed is used in Romans 11:17, 19, 23, and 24. In Strong's it is number 1461, "egkentrizo," a derivative of "Kentron" to prick or position in place. Graff is the spelling used in the King James Bible, which is correct. The modern spelling is grafted, graft which has the same meaning so as to not be confused. In the above verses, Paul uses the word meaning to prick, insert by making a puncture or small opening, to engraft. The Apostle observes that it is contrary to nature that a branch of a wild olive tree should be grafted into a good olive tree, although the opposite is done.[9]

God makes His grafting by grace, so it has to work. Paul was showing God's magnified mercy being shown to the Gentiles by grafting such a wild, pagan people into the Lord Jesus Christ, the good olive tree. If God is willing to do this, He can easily graft the natural branches (Israel) back into their own olive tree. Faith is the key to the Jewish nation's future. To be restored to their holy place in God, God demands belief in the Lord Jesus Christ as their Messiah. All the possibilities and promises indicate a glory-filled future for Israel.

Are The Jews the Same Today?

All sorts of ideas are floating around about who are the Jews and where did they originate and is the Jew of today of Semitic origin? These revisers want to so badly to prove to everyone that Jesus was not a Jew. Here we see the forces of the anti-Semite in true colors.

For the simple proof that Jesus Christ was who *He* said *He* was, we need to learn from Scripture that He was the seed of Adam, Luke 3:38. Jesus Christ was the seed of Shem, as found in Genesis 9:26 and 27. Through Shem came forth the Israelites. The seed travels through Abraham, Genesis 12:3; and of Jacob, Genesis 28:14, and of

Judah, Genesis 49:10; and of course, through David, 1 Chronicles 17: 11-14.

This is the beginning of the Semitic race. This is the pure, uninterrupted Semitic line to the virgin birth of the Lord Jesus Christ, who was indeed a Semite. This is the Jewish line, which follows the genealogy through the Diaspora and back again to the Land of Israel for the re-gathering.

Christ came according to the promise of God as Redeemer for the perpetuity of Israel. He promised to scatter His people for their disobedience.

> "And the Lord shall scatter thee among all people, from the one end of the earth even unto the other;" (Deuteronomy 28:64)

He also promised restoration as a people to lead the nations.

> "And the Lord shall make thee the head, and not the tail; and thou shalt be above only, and thou shalt not be beneath;" (Deuteronomy 28:13)

> "So all the generations from Abraham to David are fourteen generations; and from David until the carrying away unto Babylon are fourteen generations; and from the carrying away into Babylon until Christ and fourteen generations.: (Matthew 1:17)

At the destruction of the Temple in 70 A.D. and their banishment following the destruction of Jerusalem and at the end of the Bar Kokhba Revolt of 132-135 A.D., the Jews were scattered among the nations. (Deuteronomy 28:64). This huge remnant landed in Persia and Babylon, spreading to India, northward into Syria and Russia through North Africa and into Spain and elsewhere. The continuity of the Jews was guided by God through His covenants and promises.

> *"And I will establish my covenant between me and thee and thy seed after thee in their generations for an everlasting covenant,"* (Genesis 17:7).

The Jews preserved the words of God and the testimony of His name. God also chose them through which our Saviour Jesus Christ came into the world. The Diaspora Jews have not been re-gathered, and brought back into the land, although it is a smaller portion of it, and they have not accepted Jesus Christ as their Saviour as yet.

The first Zionist convention was held in August 1897. Theodor Herzl, the founder of the Zionist movement wrote:

> *"At Basle, I found the Jewish state. If I were to say this today, I would be met by universal laughter. In five years perhaps and certainly in fifty, everyone will say it."[10]*

This, of course, came true. In November, 1917, the Foreign Minister of England, wrote the Balfour Declaration, an agreement to Zionist aspirations for a Jewish state. This put the British behind the effort to establish a national home for the Jewish people.

The British drove the Ottomans out of Palestine, and in 1948 the Jewish state was born. Since then Jews have been returning from all corners of the globe.

> *"And it shall come to pass in that day, that the Lord shall set his hand again the second time to recover the remnant of his people,"* (Isaiah 11:11a)

> ... *and gather together the dispersed of Judah from the four corners of the earth.*" (Isaiah 11:12)

The first return, remember, was when God brought the remnant of Jews from Babylon and that came from the direction of the east. This second return is prophesied to be from the "four corners of the earth," or from four directions. What we have witnessed from 1948 is this very return and re-gathering. This establishment of a Jewish State has inspired and driven the increases in Jewish population in Israel.

In 1832, there were approximately 24,000 Jews in Palestine, out of a total population of 624,000. By 1914, under the impetus of what the early Zionist congresses had been able to accomplish, this number had risen to 85,000. In 1927, it had reached 150,000; in 1936, 404,000; and in 1948, when the modern state was born, 650,000.[11]

In coming home to Israel, the Jews have nearly disappeared from Muslim areas. From 1920 to 1970, 900,000 Jews were expelled from Arab and other Muslim countries.[12]

In countries such as; Egypt, Iraq, Morocco, Tunisia, Libya, Algeria, Yemen, and Iran, the Jewish populations have decreased 90-100%. This is the fulfillment of Ezekiel 37:14, "...and I shall place you in your own land:" and is in preparation for Israel's national conversion. Israel will live in immortality because of an immortal God and His eternal covenants.

In 1754, Thomas Newton wrote of the Jews;

"Their preservation is really one of the most illustrious acts of Divine Providence. They are dispersed among all nations,...they can produce their pedigree from the beginning of the world... After wars, massacres and persecutions they still subsist; they are still quite numerous. What but a supernatural power could have preserved them in such a manner as no other nation on earth has been preserved?" (Dissertation on the Prophecies, VIII, section 2)[13]

Who Is A Jew?

Abraham was first called a Hebrew in Genesis 14:13. God separated Abraham from the other nations physically and spiritually. Israelites are Hebrews that are descendants of Jacob. The physical and spiritual descendants of Jacob, also named Israel, along with Abraham and Isaac and their wives, are all Jews.

The Bible says that in the last days, the house of Jacob, or all Israel, will return. It is not known as yet to just which tribes most of the Jews belong, but God knows. It is understood that at one time all Jews belonged to the tribe of Judah, but because after the Babylonian captivity Judah was the dominant tribe, all Israelites came to be called Jews. All who have the name Cohen or the name Levi in any form in their name, belong to the tribe of Levi."...when the return is complete, all Jews will again be settled in the land according to their ancestral fathers, the 12 sons of Jacob.[14]

"And I heard the number of them which were sealed: and there were sealed a hundred and forty and four thousand of all the tribes of the children of Israel." (Revelation 7:4)

Khazar Myth

The Khazar hypothesis of Ashkenazi ancestry, often called the "Khazar Myth", says that Ashkenazi Jews are in large part descended from the Khazars, a multi-ethnic conglomerate of Turkic peoples who formed a semi-nomadic Khanate in the areas extending from Eastern Europe to Central Asia. The ruling elite of the Khazars was said by Judah Halevi and Abraham ibn David to have converted to Rabbinic Judaism.[15]

Genetic studies have shown no evidence of Khazar origins among Ashkenazi Jews, only evidence of mixed near Eastern/Mediterranean and Southern European origins. The hypothesis still finds some occasional (radical) defenders for its extreme tenets. These have anti-Zionist (anti-Semetic) leanings that challenge the idea that present day Jews have genetic ties to ancient Israel, and also has a role in anti-Semitic theories. This accusation that today's Jews are not indigenous to Israel, but that they are descendant from white Europeans is very extreme and held by a small minority of self-proclaimed "woke" preachers and the like. They are anti-Semetic and the fact that this has caught on in some "Christian" Identist circles is cause for some alarm. They are so quick to state that Jewish people are unrelated to ancient Israelites, and have no history in Israel or even a connection to the promised (by God) land.

The popularizing of the Khazar Myth was made possible by Arthus Koestler, an Atheist, who wrote in 1978 a book "The Thirteeth Tribe." The theory was rocketed into fame when a Saudi Arabian delegate to the U.N. claimed the book "negated Israel's right to exist." [16] Neo-Nazi magazine "The Thunderbolt" declared it "the political bombshell of the Century."[17]

It was later proven that Koestler was not the intellectual he understood himself to be and had no professional expertise in this subject at all. Today's science and genetic testing-prone Koestler and his central protests were wrong. The vast majority of Jews today can be genetically traced back to the Levant area, not the Khazars.[18]

Jeremiah 31:35-36 holds the promise of God that as long as the sun, moon, and stars remain in the sky there will be an Israel.

> "Thus saith the Lord, which giveth the sun for a light by day, and the ordinances of the moon and of the stars for a light by night, which divideth the sea when the waves thereof roar; the Lord of hosts in his name:
>
> If those ordinances depart from before me, saith the Lord, then the seed of Israel also shall cease from being a nation before me forever."
>
> "He hath also stablished them for ever and ever: he hath made a decree which shall not pass. (Psalm 148:6)

Sir Isaac Newton wrote out most of the scriptures which contained the promises of God about the restoration of Israel. God said He would return His people to the land since He knows the end from the beginning, and we can have complete confidence that God knows who are the real Jewish people of Israel.

Some of the so-called evidence of the Jewish Conversion of the Khazars, include the Kievan letter found in Cairo. Written in Hebrew it was found along with a collection of Jewish writings and documents. It is forbidden to throw away anything with Hebrew letters. This introductory letter bears witness to the credibility of the holder of the letter, but he probably did not even speak Hebrew. It was most likely written by a Jewish scribe in Hebrew. At the bottom of it was written in Turkic, by a Khazar Jewish official, and not knowing basic Hebrew indicates to historians that the conversion of the Khazars was most likely superficial. Very few Jewish schools were found among the Khazars, and all evidence points to a non-practice of circumcision, which is evidence of very shallow religious conversion, and that they probably remained pluralistic. Widespread Khazar influence across the Jewish Diaspora is non-existent.

God said He will and would re-gather His very own Jewish people. He does not lie and He knows who they are and where they are. To believe any different is to call God a liar. He makes sure His word since He has put His words above His name. He backs up His words and His promises, as we watch them come to pass: Jeremiah 31:35-36' Amos 9:15; Zechariah 12:10; Psalm 138.2.

The Abrahamic Covenant

Covenants For a Covenant People

God's covenant people, the Jews, were given several covenants that are between them and God. The biblical basis for defining Jewishness lies in the Abrahamic Covenant in Genesis. It is found in Genesis 12:1-3, where God says:

"And I will make of thee a great nation, and I will bless thee, and make thy name great; and thou shalt be a blessing:" (v2)

The three promises of God contained in his covenant are:

1. The land, "… unto a land that I will shew thee:"
2. A great nation with a very large, natural posterity.
3. God promised that He would bless Abraham and his posterity and those that blessed him and that all the families of the earth would be blessed through him.

God has given Israel the land as a promise.

"For all the land which thou seest, to thee will I give it, and to thy seed forever." (Genesis 13:15)

"And I will establish my covenant between me and thee and thy seed after thee in their generations for an everlasting covenant," (Genesis 17:7)

For a reaffirmation of his promise, God says:

"And I will give unto thee, and to thy seed after thee, the land wherein thou art a stranger, all the land of Canaan, for an everlasting possession, and I will be their God." (Genesis 17:8)

There are two types of covenants, conditional as well as unconditional. The Sinai, or Mosaic covenant, is a conditional covenant. It is the only conditional covenant that God made between Him and the Israelites. The conditional mosaic covenant is dependent on the response of the Israelites to

God's conditions. The Mosaic covenant contains the phrase, "Now therefore, if ye will obey my voice indeed, and keep my covenant, ..." (Exodus 19:5). It is a mutual agreement of God with man, that if the demands and things promised are fulfilled by man's obedience, special blessings are provided according to met conditions. Otherwise, failure to meet God's conditions bring definite punishment. So the conditional covenant depends for its fulfillment upon the one receiving the covenant, not on the one who makes the covenant. The "if" word is so attached.

For the unconditional covenants, the promises covenanted owe their fulfillment alone to the one making the covenant, namely God. These covenants have no "if" clause attached to them. Instead, the Almighty is direct with Israel and says, "I will" bring these promises and blessings to pass definitely. We believe that God will bring to fruition all that He says based on His authority and His integrity.

God's covenants are literal and are taken to be literally fulfilled completely. Not only have parts of the Abrahamic covenant been literally fulfilled, but every word and parts of all four major unconditional covenants will be and are expected to be literally fulfilled.

Thus, the Abrahamic Covenant is the basis, the foundation for all the great covenants made by God to come about. These unconditional covenants are eternal, with statements made in Genesis 17:7, 13, 19, 1 Chronicles 16:17; and in Psalm 105:10.[19] The Abrahamic and the other unconditional covenants were made with God's covenant people, Israel.

> *"Who are Israelites; to whom pertaineth the adoption, and the glory, and the Covenants,..."* (Romans 9:4)

Counter to that, Gentiles were without God:

> *"...being aliens from the Commonwealth of Israel, and strangers from the covenants of promise, having no hope, and without God in the world:"* (Ephesians 2:12)

However, now we as Gentiles have hope due to the shed of blood of Christ on the Cross and faith in Christ.

"Cutting a Covenant"

It is important to understand the Abrahamic Covenant to have a proper understanding of the whole Bible. It holds the key to the whole Old Testament as its fulfillment extends into the New Testament. For its provisions and their character set the whole moulage for the entire body of scriptural truth.[20] Interpretive discernment of this covenant can govern one's theological outlook. Unfortunately, importance and meaning don't always add up to agreement. The difficulty for some lies in the fact that the information connected with the Abrahamic covenant is dispersed through several chapters of Scripture and often seem repetitive in its exhibition. If each of the parts of the Covenant is carefully expounded, then the sum of its parts will be for the sake of understanding a studied comprehensive whole.

A defining of some terms will add to the comprehension of this covenant. The term, covenant, in the Hebrew being *"berit,"* is used in Genesis 15:18 and 17:1-21. The Lord's promises to Abraham are also found in Exod. 2:24; 6: 4-5; Lev 26: 42-44; and Deut. 4:31.

In the New Testament, the Greek word *"diatheke"*: in regards to the covenant is to be found in, Luke 1:72; Acts 3:25, 7:8; Gal. 3:17; 4:24.

To clear up any confusion, the word "covenant" is used five times in the New Testament, and the word "Promise", *"epangelia"* is used nineteen times, clearly referring to the Lord's word/promise to Abraham. Thus, New Testament usage raises the relationship between the words promise and covenant. There is a close relationship between the two terms, but the two terms are not synonymous. Paul uses and distinguishes the two terms in Romans 9:4.

> *"Wherein God, willing more abundantly to shew unto the heirs of promise the immutability of his counsel, confirmed it by an oath:"* (Heb. 6:17)

Hebrews 6:17 is speaking of God's perpetuity of His words of promise which He guaranteed by His covenant oath. We can simplify by stating that God, by promise, gave His intention to do a certain something for Abraham and his descendants, and to seal His oath with a binding obligation to Abraham and his seed.

Covenant Ceremony

The Abrahamic Covenant was finalized or sealed by a solemn act of God in a ritual that symbolized the shedding of blood and then passing between the parts of the sacrifice. A warning is given to those who transgress the covenant in Jeremiah 34:18. In spite of acts of disobedience on mankind's part, the promises in this covenant remain eternally.

God confirms this in Genesis 15:18.

> *"In the same day the Lord made a covenant with Abram, saying, unto thy see have I given this land,"*

The method God used to administer the covenant is conveyed by the Hebrew word, "berit," and its literal meaning is "cutting a covenant." God's first instructions to Abraham were to look to the heavens and try to count the stars, since Abraham complained he had no heir.

> *"Look now toward heaven, and tell the stars, if thou be able to number them: and he said unto him, so shall thy seed be."* (Genesis 15:6)

Through an animal service God will assure Abraham that He means every word He says about heirs, a great nation, and possession of the land.

> *"And he said unto him, take me an heifer of three years old, and a she goat of three years old, and a ram of three years old, and a turtle dove, and a young pigeon."* (Genesis 15:9)

Abraham and those around him would understand what was going on here. There were many cultures that were familiar to him as he was preparing the blood sacrifice. Ancient Mari and Alalakh texts tell of participants in the covenant, walking through the blood of the animals collected in the middle of the pieces to enact the covenant and curse ones who broke the promises.[21]

This practice was not new and was widely understood.

> *"And he took unto him all these, and divided them in the midst, and laid each piece one against the other: but the birds divided he not."* (Genesis 15:10)

Keep in mind that this ceremony was divinely given to Abraham to assure him that his seed would indeed inherit the land promised and that all the promises of God would be fulfilled. God is performing this ceremony by Himself with no conditions attached. Abraham prepared the animals so that he and God might enter into a blood covenant. By laying the pieces of the divided animals in two rows opposite each other, the preparation was completed for the participants making the covenant would be passing between them. Abraham would then be expecting to walk with God through the divided animals into a blood covenant. By binding His blood to the ritual he knew it would either fulfill the covenant or be payment for any breach of the covenant. It was not to be.

> *"And when the sun was going down, a deep sleep fell upon Abram;"* (Genesis 15:12)

God Himself is going alone through the sacrifices and Abraham is not because God is doing all the promising and Abraham is not going to do a thing. Abraham and his heirs will be receiving the promises and just believe God. No other action is needed.

This is what happened two thousand years ago as God the Father sent His son to die for the sins of the world. God the Father sacrificed His son for each and everyone's sin so that our sins would be fully paid for. Whosoever believes in the Lord Jesus Christ, appropriates His shed blood for the remission of sins. Christ went to the cross, took away the paralysis of sin so that we could be free.

So, Abraham was not a participant in the covenant, which God took upon Himself all the responsibility that would have been assumed had there been two equal participants. God walked through the blood, the blood pool or blood path, binding Himself to the fate of the sacrificed animals if there was any failure to keep the covenant.

> *"And it came to pass, that, when the sun went down, and it was dark, behold a smoking furnace, and a burning lamp that passed between those pieces:"* (Genesis 15:17)

Both the smoking furnace and the burning lamp speak of Christ Jesus. It was a Theophany of Christ, with the furnace symbolizing judgment and the lamp signifying Jesus Christ as the light of the world.

Christ says He will give the land to Abraham and his seed after spending 400 years in a strange land (Egypt). It will be the land of the Kenites, the Kenizzites, the Kadmonites, the Hittites, the Perizzites, the Rephaims, the Amorites, the Canaanites, and the Girgashites, and the Jebusites. [Gen. 15:18-21]

The Tenets of the Abrahamic Covenant: were to make of Abraham a great nation, and this would be God's chosen nation, Israel.

61

"And I will make of thee a great nation, and I will bless thee, and make thy name great; and thou shalt be a blessing: (Genesis 12:2)

In Genesis 13:16 God says that He will make Abraham's seed as the dust of the earth which no one can possibly count. God had told Abraham that His spiritual seed would be as many as the number of stars (Gen. 15:6)

"Therefore, it is of faith, that it might be by grace; to the end the promise might be sure to all the seed;...which is of the faith of Abraham; who is the father of us all," (Romans 4:16)

To this great nation God would give a land. This has already been discussed from Genesis 15:18-21, as the Promised land from the rivers of Egypt unto the Euphrates.

To these great promises was added that Abraham and the nation of Israel would be a blessing to those who bless him and a curse to them that cursed Israel. Therefore, all the families of the earth were to be blessed by the coming of the Lord Jesus Christ. Those believers would be set apart with great spiritual blessings and eternal life.

And the scripture,

." foreseeing that God would justify the heathen through faith, preached before the gospel unto Abraham, saying, in thee shall all nations be blessed." (Galatians 3:8)

"That the blessing of Abraham might come on the Gentiles through Jesus Christ; that we might receive the promise of the Spirit through faith (Galatians 3:14)

The importance of the Abrahamic Covenant cannot be overstated. If any blessings or any of the promises of this foundational covenant had been nullified, Christ would not have come, there would not be any great nation from Abraham, and thus no blessings, and there would not be any assurance of a great salvation or eternal life. If it had been a conditional covenant there would be no parts of the covenant fulfilled at any later date.

The gift of the land is modified by prophecies of three dispossessions and restorations (Gen. 15:13, 14, 16; Jer. 25:11, 12; Deut. 28:62-65; 39: 1-3). Two dispossessions and restorations have been accomplished. Israel is now in the third dispersion, from which she will be restored at the return of the Lord as King under the Davidic Covenant (Deut. 30:3; Jer. 23: 5-8; Ezk. 37: 21-25; Luke 1:30-33; Acts 15: 14-17.[22]

We know that some things in the Abrahamic Covenant have been partially fulfilled, i.e., the coming of Christ, assurance of salvation and eternal life, and spiritual blessings. Abraham had eight sons and it was revealed by God that the seed of the Saviour, the promised seed, was only through Sarah's son, Isaac. The covenant was confirmed through Jacob, Isaac's son and then through Jacob's twelve sons, who fathered the twelve tribes of Israel.

"All these are the twelve tribes of Israel:"
(Gen. 49:28a)

Thus, the Abrahamic covenant provides the biblical definition of Jewishness: a descendant of Abraham, Isaac, and Jacob.[23]

The Day of the Lord

The day of the Lord is very important and pivotal for Israel. Besides being judgment time for the Gentiles and Gentile nations, it is the final time God deals with Israel and his Jewish people. This happens in the first seven years of the day of the Lord, which then extends into the Millennial Kingdom. The Church has already gone to meet Christ in the Rapture in the clouds. (1 Thessalonians 4:17).

> *"For yourselves know perfectly that the day of the Lord so cometh as a thief in the night.* (1 Thess. 5:2)

This is not how Christ Jesus comes to the church but how it will seem to a hapless world. Christians are not waiting for an Antichrist or a thief, but the Lord and Saviour Jesus Christ. So, when the day of the Lord, which begins with Judgment, comes there will be no church around to warn all the unsaved sinners.

> *"For when they shall say, peace and safety; then sudden destruction cometh upon them, "* (1 Thess. 5:3)

The day of the Lord will be sudden and catch the world completely unaware. The day of the Lord is the period of time beginning with the 7-year Tribulation and extends through the Millennium and the 1000 year reign of Christ here on the earth. The world had been warned:

> *"Let no man deceive you by any means;"* (2 Thess. 2:3a)

> *"Remember ye not that, when I was yet with you, I told you these things?"* (2 Thess. 2:5)

64

This day has been reserved for them who would believe the world's lies that there was nothing to worry about, and that were many ways by which all could enter heaven. They could not get their eyes on Jesus and walk by faith, so the trap was set by Antichrist and the unbelievers are caught by the lies and deceit.

"And for this cause God shall send them strong delusion, that they should believe a lie." (2 Thess. 2:11)

For people who will not take a stand, to make a decision one way or the other, they are closed to the Gospel. The lost ones will refuse to hear, and if they do will refuse to accept it. God will then send them strong delusion because they received not the truth but opened up to a lie. The lie of the Antichrist that will be believed is that Jesus Christ is not who they need and He isn't who He says He is anyway. The Antichrist will flatter people, make them feel good about themselves, and invite them all to help in building a kingdom on earth with him. This is very tragic as these deceived ones will be led to believe they are entering the Millennium Kingdom when, in fact, they are plunging headlong in to the 7-year Tribulation.

"That they all might be damned who believed not the truth, but had pleasure in unrighteousness." (2 Thess. 2:12)

Jew and Gentile alike will be caught up in the lie of Antichrist. These are the three types of people in the world: the Jew, the Gentile, and the church of God.

"Give none offense, neither to the Jews, nor to the Gentiles, nor to the church of God:" (1 Corinthians 10:32)

The church will be gone from the face of the earth and with Christ during the 7-year Tribulation. The church presently is composed of saved Jews and Gentiles. What will be left during the opening of the Tribulation, the beginning of the day of the Lord, will be unsaved, unredeemed, Jewish and Gentile children of the devil.

Day of the Lord in O.T.

"For the day of the Lord of hosts shall be upon every one that is proud and lofty, and upon every one that I lifted up; and he shall be brought low. " (Isa.2:12.)

Upon the proud, those with their high and mighty thoughts of ruling the world, and to the haughtiest of men and women, there is a reckoning coming. This will be executed by God, whom they have left out in their lives.

"Behold, the day of the Lord cometh, cruel both with wrath and fierce anger, to lay the land desolate; and he shall destroy the sinners thereof out of it. (Isa. 13:9)

This is not a day anyone has yet seen. It is terrible, full of God's fierce anger, and sinners must beware and seek safety in the Lord now before it is too late. This verse is looking forward into sinners' destiny, into the great Tribulation.

"For this is the day of the Lord God of hosts, a day of vengeance, that he may avenge him of his adversaries: and the sword shall devour,..." (Jeremiah 46:10)

This is judgment upon the nations and against the adversaries of God. They have openly disregarded and poked God in the eye long enough and have made themselves a sacrifice for God. None shall escape such a fierce vengeance.

> *"For the day is near, even the day of the Lord is near, a cloudy day; it shall be the time of the heathen."* (Ezekiel 30:3)

This prophecy is contained within one about the nation of Egypt. Egypt is a type of all the nations of the world and it is pictured as a cloudy day. This is alarming somewhat in that part of the world and it needs to be taken note of. It is the time of the heathen nations to undergo judgment.

> *"Alas for the day! For the day of the Lord is at hand, and as a destruction from the almighty shall it come."* (Joel 1:15)

This verse looks directly into that day of the Lord. There are warnings all about us now; wars, shortages, viruses, etc. Man is being given a chance to heed these warnings and get saved and avoid being lost forever. We are living in our own day, man's day. It is the times of the Gentiles; "Jerusalem shall be trodden down of the Gentiles, until the times of the Gentiles be fulfilled (Luke 21:24. Man's judgment prevails and because of that the world is in a hopeless state. The day of Christ will have already come and gone, Christ will have removed the church from this earth.

Second Thessalonians 2:2 speaks of that day of Christ.

> *"That ye be not soon shaken in mind, or be troubled, neither by spirit, nor by word, nor by*

letter as from us, as that the day of Christ is at hand. (2 Thess. 2:2)

The day of Christ is a bright day, full of light for those who believe. But the day of the Lord is a dark and gloomy day. It is Tribulation that will come and bring with it destruction that has never happened before.

"For then shall be great Tribulation, such as was not since the beginning of the world to this time, no, nor ever shall be." (Matthew 24:21)

"Who shall be punished with everlasting destruction from the presence of the Lord, and from the glory of his power;" (2 Thess. 1:9).

Joel now prophesies and explains what the day of the Lord entails.

"A day of darkness and of gloominess, a day of clouds and of thick darkness, as the morning spread upon the mountains: a great people and a strong; (Joel 2:2)

This is the grim picture of the Great Tribulation in full swing, something you do not want to be a part of and from which there will not be a chance of escape. The day of the Lord begins with darkness, and is darkness. This is the day of Doom and Gloom, and thick darkness.

"And Moses stretched forth his hand toward heaven; and there was a thick darkness in all the land of Egypt three days:" (Exodus 10:22)

The thick darkness was the next to the last plague that God brought upon Pharaoh, and on Egypt. Each person could not see the next, and none of the Egyptians could get up nor move for three whole days. The Egyptians were in darkness but the children of Israel had light.

> *"Woe unto you that desire the day of the Lord! To what end is it for you? The day of the Lord is darkness, and not light."* (Amos 5:18)

The question that is asked by God is easily answered by a verse in the book of John.

> *"And this is the condemnation, that light is come into the world, and men loved darkness rather than light, because their deeds were evil."* (John 3:19).

If you are not saved and are not a child of God, desiring a day that begins in darkness and offers no escape is not a very smart decision to make. Your end is determined and the outlook is catastrophic. The day of the Lord starts in darkness with Christ's judgment and then moves to the second coming of Christ who establishes His Kingdom here on earth. You have truly got to love darkness to keep your ugly, evil deeds to remain unrevealed. So, Amos is warning Jews here. Do not think that ritualistic worship and celebrating the feasts in the course of a year is a remedy for being redeemed by the blood of Christ. Do not expect Christ to pass over you if His blood is not on the lintels of your door. Desiring such a dark, blood-letting day is not only not desirable but insanely deadly.

> *"I hate, I despise your feast days, and I will not smell in your solemn assemblies."* (Amos 5:21)

God does not accept blind faith or dishonesty. If you are living a sinful life, and going through mosaic rituals of idolatry, know that God rejects that and will not use that. If you have to say that you worship false gods and things of the flesh, be prepared for God's wrath of judgment.

> *"For the day of the Lord is near upon all the heathen: as thou hast done, it shall be done unto thee: thy reward shall return upon thine own head."* (Obadiah 15)

Remember that the technical term Day of the Lord begins right after the Rapture of the Church, with the 7-year Tribulation and continues through the Millennium. The Day of the Lord is near, and it will be upon all the nations and their impending judgment. In discussing the judgment of nations, Obadiah 15 is set in the judgment of God on the nation of Edom. It is very possible Edom and other ancient nations will become a nation once more and face their judgment.

> *"Who is this that cometh from Edom,...I have trodden the winepress alone; for I will tread them in my anger,... for the day of vengeance is in mine heart, and the year of my redeemed is come:* (Isaiah 63:1-4)

Edom, and the rest of the ancient nations, together with all of today's nations will not escape God's judgment during the Day of the Lord. What was to come about for Edom finally did come about, for they were destroyed by Babylon and others. The Romans finished them off and if they reappear again Christ will lead any who repent into the Kingdom with Him. All nations will qualify for judgment for what they have done; and Christ said that it shall be done back unto them. In the Day of the Lord is when their reward will be returned upon their own head.

Zephaniah uses the term Day of the Lord seven times in his prophecy. There are other uses of it in different terms but which have the same meaning. Day of the Lord pertains to the Tribulation period and includes the time of the Millennial Kingdom. Here is presented the darker side of the love of God in the form of judgment and in a very harsh, politically incorrect for our day, manner. Even though the Day of the Lord is not necessarily used everywhere in Zephaniah, a strong reference to it can be clearly understood with use of other terms.

> *"That day is a day of wrath, a day of trouble and distress, a day of wasteness and desolation, a day of darkness and gloominess, a day of clouds and thick darkness.* (Zephaniah 1:15)

> *"the great day of the Lord is near, it is near, and hasteth greatly, even the voice of the day of the Lord: the might man shall cry there bitterly.* (Zephaniah 1:14)

This is the great Day of the Lord depicting the Great Tribulation. This is judgment on the sinful rejection of God by Judah but is just a small precursor to the near future Tribulation. Their peace is now shattered with no hope for them until Jesus comes again. In Verse 14 Zephaniah bring out the raw harshness of the day with descriptive couplets. It has trouble and distress. In Jeremiah 30:7 it is written that that day is great and that none is like it, it is a time of Jacob's Trouble, God's time of judgment the world will be judged and a separation is made between God-fearing and unbelieving Jews. Distress is a near helpless state of anxiety and acute suffering and being in need of immediate assistance.

Wasteness is from Hebrew, *"Shoah"*, to rush over, a tempest, a storm. This awful time will have destructive storm-like qualities. It is by no means a pleasant time as everything will be swept away. Desolation is the Hebrew word, *"mshowah"* meaning the wrecking act has taken place and all that's left is ruin, desolation and wasted places. It will not be a pretty sight by any means.

Along with the darkness and gloominess, together with a day of clouds, and thick darkness, we get a picture of great wrath and judgment from God, but it has within it the love of God. He must punish the evil to be the one true God, so He can do good to His creatures. The cycle of sin, suffering, disease, sorrow, and death will finally be broken and a great Tribulation is God's way of doing so.

> *"Behold, the day of the Lord cometh, and thy spoil shall be divided." in the midst of thee."*
> (Zechariah 14:1)

We are dealing with the second coming of the Lord Jesus Christ and the Day of the Lord. It affects the whole population of Jews in Israel at the time of the Tribulation as Christ prepares the ones who will be gathered by Him into the Millennial Kingdom. This again is end of the age prophecy and looks into the future. People need to take notice, for the Day of the Lord cometh. You cannot stop it, God said it will be here, it is inevitable. It is a day that everyone can be certain will come, sometime in the future when the Church has been removed. Any spoil you may be hoarding, all things that you have, will be taken and divided and ransacked. As the next verse tells us, the houses will be rifled, the women raped, and only half the city of Jerusalem will survive. We find out later that in the Tribulation only one-third of the Jews will escape Antichrist.

"Behold, I will send you Elijah the prophet before the coming of the great and dreadful Day of the Lord. (Malachi 4:5).

The terrible day of the Lord will be announced, but who will listen?

So, we know that when the Day of the Lord comes it will be a 7-year time of trouble for unsaved Gentiles and the Jews of Israel. This period is described as having characteristics and events which remain to be fulfilled and which cannot be fulfilled until the Church has been raptured. It will be an unprecedented time in the world's history of intense trouble bringing the forces of evil to a destructive climax and then will come the Millennial Kingdom.

For the nation Israel the Tribulation will be for the purpose of cleansing in preparation for entering the Millennial Kingdom. Even after such a painful and sinful history, for Israel this Tribulation stands alone in its character and severity. These trials and severe persecutions will try the nation, finally yielding the Tribulation remnant which will be and be protected by the Lord. Antichrist will try to kill the Jews who are fleeing but the Lord Jesus Christ will save and protect them. For the nation Israel, one-third will come through the fire, tested and tried. They will be delivered at its conclusion by the return of their promised Messiah, the Lord Jesus

Christ. Christ will lead them out of their hidden safe place. They will acknowledge their Lord and Saviour Jesus Christ and become the head of the nations in the Millennial Kingdom.

> *"Alas! For that day is great, so that none is like it: it is even the time of Jacob's trouble; but he shall be saved out of it."* (Jeremiah 30:7)

The true church, the body of Christ, does not enter the Tribulation. The main body of the book of Revelation does not mention the true Church as being present during the Tribulation. Since the presence of the apostate Church during the Tribulation is one of its characteristics, the presence of the genuine Church is not necessary. Any Jew today that receives Jesus Christ as Saviour then becomes part of the True Church. All who are saved Jews in this age are truly part of the Church as are saved Gentiles.

Kingdom

There are specifics involved with the doctrine of the Kingdom, one of them in particular affecting the Jews.

The Kingdom of God includes all of God's intelligent beings which are in heaven or on earth and are subjects of God. Kingdom in Greek is *"basileia,"* a realm, kingdom. The eternal kingdom of God was prophesied and promised to Israel through David the King.

> *"And thine house and thy kingdom shall be established forever before thee: thy throne shall be established for ever.:* (2 Samuel 7:16)

"He shall be great, and shall be called the Son of the Highest: and the Lord God shall give unto him the throne of his father David:

And he shall reign over the house of Jacob forever; and of his kingdom there shall be no end." (Luke 1:32, 33)

It is a kingdom that is coming and with power.

"And in the days of these kings shall the God of heaven set up a kingdom, which shall never be destroyed. (Daniel 2:44)

The Millennial Kingdom which will be set up by the Lord Jesus is to be the rule of Christ on earth which distances itself from a spiritual reign in the hearts of men. The reign of Christ on earth is the righteous government of Christ.

"But with righteousness shall he judge the poor, and reprove with equity for the meek of the earth: and he shall smite the earth with the rod of his mouth, and with the breath of his lips shall be slay the wicked." (Isaiah 11:4)

"And in that day there shall be a root of Jesse, which shall stand for an ensign of the people; to it shall the Gentiles seek; and his rest shall be glorious (Isaiah 11:10)

The Gentiles, who have come through the Tribulation, in many countries, and have gotten saved, will have a place in the Millennial Kingdom. But for Israel, they have been guided and promised the Kingdom for over three thousand years. They will be the head of all nations and not the tail. They will be a united nation.

"...and will gather them on every side, and bring them into their own land;

And I will make them one nation in the land upon the mountains of Israel; and one king shall be king to them all: and they shall no more be two nations, neither shall they be divided into two kingdoms any more at all. (Ezekiel 37:21-22)

All the tribes of Israel will be present in the Millennium, and they will become one nation again, and not two, as before. All the people of Israel will live upon the mountains if Israel; and they will be in their own land, and will be separate from the other nations under their Messiah, the Lord Jesus Christ. This is the land given to Jacob, God's servant, and wherein his fathers have dwelt.

"And they shall dwell in the land that I have given unto Jacob my servant, ...even they and their children, and their children's children for ever: and my servant David shall be their prince forever," (Ezekiel 37:25)

David will be their king and will rule over all the tribes of Israel as they will be restored as a nation under the Lord Jesus Christ. They will walk in the judgments of God, observe God's statutes, and do them.

There will be no mistake about who is in charge.

"And I will set up one shepherd over them, and he shall feed thee, even my servant David;" (Ezek. 34:23)

David will be the Chief under-shepherd of all Israel, including all the Tribes, and they and the rest of the Millennium world will be ruled by the Lord Jesus Christ.

"Afterward shall the children of Israel return, and seek the Lord their God," (Hosea 3:5)

"In that day will I raise up the Tabernacle of David that is fallen, and close up the breaches thereof;" (Amos 9:11a)

Christ will be the Chief Shepherd and rule the nations.

"Now the God of peace, that brought again from the dead our Lord Jesus, that great shepherd of the sheep, through the blood of the everlasting covenant." (Hebrews 13:20)

What is the Gospel?

Unrepentant Jews and unsaved Gentiles need to believe the Gospel and be saved in order to enter the Kingdom of heaven with the Lord Jesus Christ. Jews and Gentiles that are saved in the present Age of Grace will be part of the church as the Bride of Christ.

What does it mean to believe the Gospel: What exactly is the Gospel? There are five essential points that are helpful in understanding what the Gospel is and how to get saved:

1. First, a person has to repent. In order to repent a person has to understand that he/she is a sinner (Romans 3:10-11,23). That person who believes that there is nothing wrong, cannot repent.

2. A person must realize that if repentance does not take place, that person will face God's judgment for sin: hell (Rom.. 6:23; Revelations 21:8)

77

3. In order for one to come to Christ, who Christ is must be realized; that he is eternal God (John 1: 1, 14; Col. 2:9).
4. An unsaved person must totally depend on the atoning work of Christ on the Cross that has been payment for a sinner's sins. There is no other possible work that can be done for the forgiveness of sin, other than what Christ has done. (1 Peter 3:18; Luke 24:1-7)
5. One Must believe that Christ died for the sins of the world, and rose again from the dead. (Matthew 28:1-8; Luke 24: 1-7).

If a person believes in these five points of the Gospel, that Christ died and paid the penalty for everyone's sins, and truly has repented, then that person will be saved. If there is any denied or rejection of Christ's redeeming work of salvation, then there is only rejection to damnation for that soul.

Gospel

> *"And I saw another angel fly in the midst of heaven, having the everlasting gospel to preach unto them that dwell on the earth, and to every nation, and kindred, and tongue, and people."* (Revelation 14:6)

The word gospel simply means "good news." What is contained in that good news is that God's son, the Lord Jesus Christ died for all man's sins, that he was buried, and that he rose again to be the risen Saviour. Paul says:

"For I delivered unto you first of all that which I also received, how that Christ died for our sins according to the scriptures;

And that he was buried, and that he rose again the third day according to the scriptures:" (1 Corinthians 15: 3, 4)

Every Christian and saved person has been commanded to spread the gospel or good news.

"And he said unto them, go ye into all the world, and preach the gospel to every creature.: (Mark 16:15)

In Scofield's Bible four forms of the Gospel are listed.

The first is the Gospel of the kingdom. This gospel is the good news that the Lord Jesus will bring in a kingdom on the earth. This is in fulfillment of the Davidic Covenant; "and when thy days be fulfilled, and thou shalt sleep with thy fathers, I will set up thy seed after thee, which shall proceed out of thy bowels, and I will establish his kingdom" (2 Sam. 7:12). David's kingdom will be in the land, Israel, and it will be forever. It is political, spiritual, of Israel, and universal. It will have King David on the throne under God's son, Jesus Christ, the King of Kings and be for one thousand years.

The first part of the preaching of the Gospel of the Kingdom was begun with John the Baptist, continued by Christ Jesus when He was on earth and finished for the past with the rejection of that gospel and the king.

"In those days came John the Baptist, preaching in the wilderness of Judea,

And saying, repent thee, for the kingdom of heaven is at hand." (Matthew 3:1, 2)

The next preaching of this kingdom Gospel is yet future.

"And this gospel of the kingdom shall be preached in all the world for a witness unto all nations; and then shall the end come." (Matthew 24:14)

There is some, maybe a lot, of confusion and misuse of the terms Kingdom of Heaven and Kingdom of God. It may stem from the use of Kingdom of Heaven being used mainly in Matthew's gospel and not in any of the other gospels at all. It is all the same word in Greek, basileia (s), a noun meaning Royal dominion or kingdom. Kingdom of heaven is peculiar to Matthew as previously stated and used thirty-two times in his gospel. [24] The phrase in Matthew is, "Basileia Tonouranon," The Kingdom of Heaven. The other gospel writers use, "Basileia tou theou," the Kingdom of God.[25] It should be noted that Matthew uses "Kingdom of God" in MT. 12:28; 19:24; 21:31, 43. It refers to Daniel's prophecy in Daniel 2:44, and Daniel 7:14;

"And there was given him dominion, and glory, and a kingdom,... his dominion is an everlasting dominion, which shall not pass away, and his kingdom that which shall not be destroyed."

It is said to denote the spiritual and external kingdom which is to subsist first in more imperfect circumstances here on earth, but afterwards will appear complete in the World of Glory.[26]

"When the son of man shall come in his glory, and all the holy angels with him, then shall he sit upon the throne of his glory." (Matthew 25:31).

The prophesies given in the Old Testament of the reign of the Messiah will be an age of true righteousness. The Jews would give these a temporal meaning for their Messiah coming in the clouds, establishing a kingdom with their king. This king needed to restore their ancient religion, restore their worship, reform morals, remit their sins, be free from adversaries, and be ruled with peace and in the Messiah's glory.

Getting back to the specter of the Kingdom of God and the Kingdom of Heaven, Vine's states thus: the two are sometimes identical, yet the one term cannot be used indiscriminately for the other. In the "Kingdom of Heaven," heaven is an antithesis to earth, and the phrase is limited to the kingdom in its earthly aspect for the time being, and is used only dispensationally and in connection with Israel. In the "Kingdom of God," in its broader aspect, God is in antithesis to 'man' or 'the world' and the term signifies the entire sphere of God's rule and action in relation to the world.[27]

We find Paul spending vast amount of time disputing and expounding the things about the Kingdom of God (Acts 19:8). Paul preached on and elaborated on the things of God's Kingdom, "For a great door and effectual is open unto me," (1 Corinthians 16:9).

Gospel of the Grace of God

The second form of the Gospel is the Gospel of the grace of God. This gospel (they are all the same, just different names and preachers) is the good news of Jesus Christ and salvation by grace. Christ, the rejected King died on the cross for all sinners, was buried, and rose again from the dead for out justification.

> *"...It is the power of God unto salvation to everyone that believeth; to the Jew first, and also to the Greek."* (Romans 1:16)

> *"For he is out peace, who hath made both one, and hath broken down the middle wall of partition between us."* (Ephesians 2:14)

Through the blood of the Lord Jesus Christ we can be saved, Jew or Gentile and rest in the grace of Christ. The partition is broken down, there is now no difference between Jew and Gentile in Christ.

> *"There is neither Jew nor Greek,...ye are all one in Christ Jesus.":* (Galatians 3:28)

> *"Where there is neither Greek nor Jew,... But Christ is all, and in all."* (Colossians 3:11)

The saved Jew and saved Gentile have become Christians, together in salvation, which is in three tenses. First, the Christian has been saved from the guilt and penalty of sin, having been paid by Jesus Christ. Second, the Christian is presently being saved from dominion and living in sin. Last, the Christian will be saved at the reappearing of the Lord, from all the bodily and spiritual results of sin.

The Everlasting Gospel

"Euaggelion", the Greek for gospel, is the good news, glad tidings. It is the means, by faith, that the darkness of death surrounding man can be lifted into the light of salvation.

> *"And I saw another angel fly in the midst of heaven, having the everlasting gospel to preach unto them that dwell on the earth, and to every nation, and kindred, and tongue, and people,"* (Revelation 14:6)

In the midst of Great Tribulation, a merciful God is giving all peoples, all nations, a final chance at hearing the gospel directly from heaven.

> *"In hope of eternal life, which God, that cannot lie, promised before the world began;"* (Titus 1:2)

> *"And to make all men see what is the fellowship of the mystery, which from the beginning of the world hath been hid in God, who created all things by Jesus Christ:"* (Ephesians 3:9)

As the world as created is coming to an end, and the Great Commission has run its course, in order to dispel much misunderstanding as to what is the gospel of Jesus Christ, God is reiterating the true gospel. Too much glorifying man through science, false preaching, humanism, and serving the creature more than the creator, has made this necessary. God is making sure that the true gospel, more specifically the everlasting gospel is preached. The great burden of the gospel, a final chance being extended is, that man get back to the faith, to the one true God, the creator of all things in heaven and on earth.

If it is not about Christ, and the accepting of his saving grace, then it will end up as "another gospel" and "another Jesus" that is being preached.

Presenting a sin-bearing, crucified, resurrected Jesus Christ as Saviour; the soon to come King of kings, omnipotent Creator, then it is truly the everlasting gospel being presented.

The timing for this everlasting gospel to go out is at the very end of the Tribulation and immediately before the judgment of the nations. It has a burden of judgment and not salvation.

"My Gospel"

> *"In the day when God shall judge the secrets of men by Jesus Christ according to my gospel."* (Rom. 2:16)

Jesus Christ will judge the secrets in men's hearts even though that repugnant thought is stunning, nevertheless it will not stop, or even slow down sinful beings.

> *"...that is, the word of faith, which we preach;"* (Rom. 10:8)

> *"...how beautiful are the feet of them that preach the gospel of peace, and bring good tidings of good things!"* (Romans 10:15)

Paul was the head of Judaism, going around and rounding up Christians, whom he hated. But God called Paul by his grace;

> *"To reveal his son in me, that I might preach him among the heathen:"* (Galatians 1:16)

> *"...but I went into Arabia, and returned again unto Damascus. Then after three years I went up to Jerusalem..."* (Galatians 1:17, 18a)

The Gospel that Paul was given was not after man, but Christ Jesus.

"For I neither received it of man, neither was I taught it, but by the revelation of Jesus Christ." (Galatians 1:12)

Paul, having been separated by Jesus Christ from the Jews' religion, preached grace in the new dispensation of grace. We can say that Christ had schooled Paul in the desert in a more full development of the grace of God and told him he was to take the Gospel to the heathen, or Gentiles in the power of the Holy Ghost. It would include the out calling of the Church, the Church's relationships, position, privileges, and responsibility.

Jewish Chiliasm

"Chiliasm" is a Greek word, not an Old Testament word, meaning one thousand, referring to and is complimentary to the doctrine of the Millennium. It also refers to the thousand year kingdom age which is still yet future, and is the anticipation of the hope that Jesus Christ will return to earth to reign as King for a thousand years.

The early church believed in Chiliasm, a belief in the literal thousand year reign of Christ.

"And he laid hold on the dragon, that old serpent, which is the Devil, and Satan, and bound him a thousand years," (Revelation 20:2)

This is the removal and incarceration of Satan and it changes the earth from a place of darkness and wickedness to one of light. It clears the path for the bringing in of the kingdom. The doctrine of a future thousand year reign of Christ here on earth affects the interpretation of the implementation of the Abrahamic Covenant to Israel. The Covenant promised the land to Israel to be a fulfillment through Abraham, his physical seed, and to the spiritual seed contained in both the Old Testament and New Testament. This provision of the Promised Land for their possession for all posterity, as long as the sun and moon continue is prophetic truth.

> *"Thus saith the Lord, which giveth the sun for a light by day, and the ordinances of the moon and of the stars for a light by night,*
>
> *If those ordinances depart from before me, saith the Lord, then the seed of Israel also shall cease from being a nation before me forever.* (Jeremiah 31:35-36)

It must be restated that the promises God made to the nation of Israel will ultimately be fulfilled in the future reign that Christ will have over them. According to the pre-millennial understanding of Scripture, it makes it clear that Christ's present purpose is to call out a people, both Jew and Gentile, to form His Body, the Church.

> *"And I say unto thee, that thou art Peter, and upon this rock (Christ) I will build my church;"* (Matthew 16:18)
>
> *"And hath put all things under his feet, and gave him to be head over all things to the Church."* (Ephesians 1:22)

Christ will return before the thousand years and mark those years with his physical presence throughout, exercising his authority on earth.

Chiliasm is characterized by a thousand years which intervenes between the first and second of humanity's resurrections."[28]

(Revelation 20:5)

> *"But every man in his own order: Christ the first fruits; afterward they that are Christ's at his coming."* (1 Corinthians 15:23)

> *"Then cometh the end, when he shall have delivered up the kingdom to God, even the Father.*

> *when he shall have put down all rule and all authority and power."* (1 Corinthians 15:24)

The thousand year reign, or Millennium, was a fact held by evangelical teachers until a few hundred years ago, until now there are three held Millennial theories. Postmillennialism formed through the teachings of Englishman Daniel Whitby. He postulated that the church and other agencies would correct this evil world system and pave the way for the coming of Christ to set up His Kingdom. It has subsequently taken much too long for this theory to be upheld. This largely spurred the development of theory number two, namely, Amillennialism. Amillennialism incorporates spiritualizing the Scriptures and has engendered much popularity because of this. Any interpreter of Scripture can change and mold God's words to his or her fancy to conform to any system of interpretation. The first successful opposition to premillennialism came from the adoption of spiritualizing the principles of interpretation.[29] This system in the hands of the Alexandrians turned so radical that it undermined not only millennial doctrine but every other Christian doctrine as well. Along came Augustine to give reason to such outlandish views of interpretation. It was Augustine

87

whose system of interpretation in a non-literal way, allegorizing, which soon became known as amillennialism. His viewpoint became the doctrine of the Roman Catholic Church and many Reformers.

The basic Augustinian teaching and the main tenet of amillennialism is that the Roman Church is God's Kingdom on earth and that the Millennium is fulfilled therein. This is definitely a re-interpretation of Revelation 20:1-6, denying it as the age of the reign of Jesus Christ here on earth. His interpretation put the millennium in the inter-advent time period, with no literal fulfillment of the covenants and promises to Israel.

Early adherence to premillennialism suffered at the hands of the Romish Church. As George Peters states in "The Theocratic Kingdom;" Chiliasm disappeared in proportion as Roman Papal Catholicism advanced. The Papacy took to itself, as a robbery, that glory which is an object of hope, and can only be reached by obedience and humility of the cross. When the Church became a harlot, she ceased to be a bride who goes out to meet her bridegroom.[30]

When Christ has vanquished all enemies, there will begin a reign of peace, lasting for one thousand years, which will happen before the last judgment and the future Kingdom.. It will be the dominion of the Lord Jesus Christ reigning with His risen saints over the world and a restored Jewish nation. A Jewish Chiliasm includes a hope for a restored nation of Israel, a rebuilt temple, and a completely holy city of Jerusalem.

[1] Thou Shalt keep them", Brandenburg, editor. P 113.

[2] Inspiration for this section comes from: Garry Knighton. "Ten reasons why the nation of Israel fell (apostasy). "Heartofgod.org. 10-2018.

[3] Price. "The coming Antichrist." p.12
[4] Dr. Alva J. McClain. "Daniel's Prophecy of the 70 weeks." p 24.
[5] Dr. Noah Hutchings. "Seventy Prophetic Weeks of Daniel." p. 16.
[6] [Chapter 29, Charles Larkin, "The Trees Israel compared to." Blueetterbible.org/study/Larkin/dt/29]
[7] [Unger's Bible Dictionary. Vine. P 1158.]

[8] [Stifler, "Epistle to the Romans." p. 193]
[9] [Zodhiates, Spiros. "The Complete Word Study Dictionary NT. P 499]
[10] [Kirban, "Israel, It's Coming Tragedy.: pp 43-47]
[11] [Wood, "The Bible and Future Events." pp 20-21]
[12] [Cloud, David. "The Jews are Gone." 2019. Wayoflife.org.]
[13] [Cloud, "Israel is Evidence." Wayoflife.org 2018]
[14] {Hutchings, "Israel and the Great Synagogue." pp 27, 28].
[15] [Wikipedia,, "Khazar Hypothesis." Wikipedia.org., Khazar hypothesis]
[16] [Oneforisrael, "are Jews Genetically Descended." Oneforisrael.org.]
[17] [ibid.]
[18] [ibid]
[19] [Pentecost, "Things to Come.: p 69]
[20] [Valvoord. "Millennial Kingdom.: p 139]
[21] [Vander Laan. "Ceremony in Genesis 15." Anchorsaway.org. p 2]
[22] [Scofield Bible, 1917. Notes. Genesis 15. p 25]
[23] [Fruchtenbaum. "Israelology Part 1 of 6." galaxie.com/ctsj 05-02-02. pp 32-34]
[24] [Zodhiates. "N.T. Word Study Dictionary.: p 325.]
[25] [Ibid.]

26 [Ibid. p 325]

27 Vine's. World Bible.Iowa. p 296]

28 [Chafer, Systematic theology. Vol 3. P 264]

29 [Walvoord. "The Millennial Kingdom." P.60]

30 Peters, George. "Theocratic Kingdom." P 499]

CHAPTER 1

THE CAPTIVITIES OF ISRAEL & JUDAH

The Two Captivities and Returns

There have been two main dispersions of the Jews and two re-gatherings with a Tribulation dispersion pending.

The first, referred to as a forced exile, was prophesied by Amos in Chapter 4:2.

> *"The Lord God hath sworn by his holiness, that, Lo, the days shall come upon you, that he will take you away with hooks, and your posterity with fishhooks."*

Amos spoke this around 764 B.C., and it was about 30 years later that the northern kingdom of Israel and its ten tribes were sent into Assyrian Exile.

> *"Therefore now shall they go captive with the first that go captive, and the banquet of them that stretched themselves shall be removed."* (Amos 6:7)

They in Samaria they had been living it up, communed with sinful kingdoms around them, feasting on sumptuous meats and drinking wine in merriment. It was time for the judgment of the 10 tribes of the northern kingdom.

> *"And the God of Israel stirred up the spirit of Pul king of Assyria, and the spirit of Tilgath-Pilneser, King of Assyria, and he carried them away, even the Reubanites, and the Gadites, and the half tribe of Manasseh, and brought them unto*

Halah, and Habor, and Hara, and to the river Gozan, unto this day." (1 Chronicles 5:26)

This started in 732 B.C. In 725 B.C. Hoshea, king of Samaria, paid no honor to Assyria, therefore, the king of Assyria bound and locked away the king of Samaria.

"In the ninth year of Hoshea the king of Assyria took Samaria, and carried Israel away into Assyria,..." (2 Kings 17:6)

It was the later Assyrian rulers Sargon II and his successor (son) , Sennacherib, who were finishing off the conquest of 20 years of the northern ten tribes of Israel.

Assyrian cuneiform states that 27,290 captives were taken from Samaria.[31] Samaria was the capitol of the northern kingdom of Israel, and the conqueror was Sargon II. Sargon records his victory on the walls of his royal palace:

In my first year of reign...the people of Samaria...to the number of 27,290...I carried away...the city I rebuilt. I made it greater than it was before. People of the lands I had conquered I settled therein.[32]

Samaria had been besieged for three years, its capture to be the first achievement of the great Sargon. The year after this fall brought Sargon to invade and subdue resistance in the west. This was due to a general rising by Hamath and Sib'u. Sargon moved swiftly, a rapid march southwards brought him into contact with the Egyptian army, whom he defeated at Rapihu, some fifteen miles south of Giza. Sib'u, as Sargon says, fled in panic and was never heard of again. Sargon then marched northwards, met the king of Hamath and his allies at Karkar. He inflicted complete defeat on the allies, captured the city of Karkar, and flayed alive the king of Hamath. But there is no further mention of Samaria, and it seems clear that Israel had ceased to trouble the Assyrians.[33]

<u>Return</u>

2 Kings 15:29 tells us that Tiglath Pileser, king of Syria, took his Jewish captives from Samaria to Assyria. Sargon took away fifty chariots and 27,290 captives and, according to 2 Kings 17:6, settled them in various parts of Mesopotamia.

It can be said, with no objection, that there was no return of any type of Jewish Remnant from the northern ten tribes as a result of the Assyrian captivity. There was never a foreign edict put out to grant permission to Jews for the rebuilding of Samaria or the northern kingdom is why. In the meantime, Assyria was conquered by Babylon, which was conquered by the Medes and Persians.

> The historical accuracy by the prophet Ezra is complete only when the details of the Apocrypha's 1st and 2nd Esdras are referenced, since this is where the complete history of the dispersion of the northern kingdom of tribes is found. (2 Esdras 13: 40-48).[34]

Anything from the non-canonical Apocrypha is not accepted here and is beyond the scope of this writing. Feel welcomed to exercise such a giant leap of faith to embrace such discourses.

Since the Holy Ghost found it of any consequence to mention the Remnant return from the ten tribe's exile, has given rise to innumerable speculations, suppositions, and mythical stories about where they all ended up. Some of the places where their descendants ended up include: the coast of Guinea, the Indian tribes in America, in England, etc.

One interesting idea is that Afghanis derive their own descent from the Jews. Mr. H. Van Sittart postulates this in his "History of the Afghans.[35] Clarke added his own conjecture; I think it by far the most probable that the Afghans are the descendants of the Jews, who were led away captives by the Assyrian kings.[36]

One thing is for sure, this captivity ended the kingdom of Israel which lasted 254 years. It spanned this time from the death of Solomon, where Jeroboam led the ten tribes who split from Judah, until the taking of Samaria by Shalmaneser.

> *"Therefore, the Lord was very angry with Israel, and removed them out of his sight: there was none left but the tribe of Judah only." (2 Kings 17:18)*

The philosophical approach to history is secular society's attempt to interpret civilizations according to their flow, following so-called predictable patterns. Each civilization has a beginning, an infancy, childhood, adolescence, maturity, old age, and at last, death. Prussian philosopher-historian Oswald Spengler was such a believer. He predicted in "The Decline of the West," that western civilization was in its winter cycle and would die out by the 23rd century. [37] The survival of the Jews did not fit Spengler's theory, so he just ignored the Jews altogether. Of course, it was and is the hand of God supporting His people and His nation, Israel. The Jewish state had been founded by God at Mt. Sinai in 1200 B.C. After their fate of being carried off into Assyria, the ten tribes never again appear in the pages of history. Usually, a captured state just exchanged one set of idols for another and adopted the views and ideas and morals of their conquerors and assimilated.

Why was it so different to be captives of Assyria and not re-emerge as re-newers of a Jewish nation, than it was as we shall see, to be under the Babylonian captivity for Judah? Well, we see in history that Assyrian policy was geared to break up conquered groups into smaller groups and destroy any previous national unity. The ten tribes had succumbed to a triple threat to her existence. The first was to Israel's religion and turning from the one true God to worshipping idols. The rich were oppressing the poor, and the third threat was that intermarriage was destroying their racial purity.

Endangered by loss of Jewish identity and racial purity, idolatry, and immorality, the unity that would have continued to hold them together as a nation was gone. So, this is what happened to the ten tribes of northern Israel. What was happening in the south with the Kingdom of Judah?

The second phase of the first expulsion of all the Jews from their land that God gave them, began with God telling Judah to beware of impending judgment.

> *"Yet the lord testified against Israel, and against Judah, by all the prophets, and by all the seers, saying, Turn ye from your evil ways,..."* (2 Kings 17:13)

Judah had been reproached over and over at the same time God was warning the northern Kingdom of Israel.

British-Israel Theory[38] (2 Sam 2:9)

1. British and American People are 10 tribes of Israel.
2. Britain is Ephraim and America Is Manasseh.
3. All promises made to Israel being fulfilled with Britain and America and never with Jews.
4. Royal family of Britain true legal heirs to throne of David through Zedekiah's daughter, throne of England is throne of David. (note 2Sam. 7:16)
5. Coronation stone of England was originally Jacob's pillow.
6. There is a vital distinction between Israel and the Jews; that they are not the same kind of people, and have a different destiny.
7. Terms Israel, Judah, Jews, the house of Israel, and House of Judah never used interchangeably in scripture.
8. That Israel of Isaiah, Jeremiah and the other prophets had no tribe of Judah in it.
9. The Jews descended from the tribe of Judah only.
10. It is erroneous to call the Jews of today Israel; and the house of Israel is not Jewish.
11. The 10 tribes were lost and whoever they are, are not Jews.
12. Not once in Bible does the term Israel refer to Jews exclusively, for although Jews may be a part of Israel, Israelites are not Jews.

13.	The returning exiles from Babylon under Ezra and Nehemiah were Jews only, and not Israel.

14.	Israel left their own land, taken into captivity by the Assyrians; that they were never to return and never did; and that Israel then began to abide many days without a king (Hos. 3:4).

15.	The Jews of N.T. were only from Judah, Benjamin, and Levi.

16.	The 10 tribes were to remain lost as to identity until the very last day in which we live.

17.	Christ is not coming to a non-existent throne, but to one that now exists.

18.	David's throne is to be transferred to the 10 tribes.

19.	Because Israel lost the Sabbath, the sign which identified them as Israel, they lost their identity and national name, becoming known as Gentiles.

20.	Israel was to have a new land northwest of Palestine, on islands, and would move no more.

21.	Israel was to be punished for 2500 years, from 721 B.C. to 1800 A.D., then identified and blessed above all other people on earth.

22.	That because Anglo-Saxons are so great, powerful, and rich, they must be the 10 tribes or the whole house of Israel.

10 Tribes Theories Challenged[39]

As for some theories of where the 10 tribes would end up and where they did end up, God has something to say to us.

Israel, the 10 tribes, was to lose all trace of her lineage and be blind to her origin.

> *"...call his name Loammi: for ye are not my people, and I will not be your God.*
>
> *Yet the number of the children of Israel shall be as the sand of the sea...that in the place where it was said unto them, Ye are not my people, there it shall be said unto them, Ye are the sons of the living God."* (Hosea 1:9,10)
>
> *"For I will take away the names of Baalim out of her mouth, and they shall no more be remembered by their name.* (Hosea 2:17)
>
> *"And I will bring the blind by a way that they knew not; I will lead them in paths they have not known:"* (Isaiah 42:16a)

They were cut off as God's people, not for the losing of their identity as Israelites, because Hosea 1:11 says that the Children of Judah and the Children of Israel will be gathered together as one people once again. The names of Baal, the false gods they once worshipped instead of God, will not be remembered, forever. The cut off Jews would be spiritually blind until they receive Jesus as their Messiah at the end of the Tribulation when they will enter the Kingdom.

In the book of Daniel the captives from Jerusalem, of which he was one, are named as being children of Israel.

Nebuchadnezzar spoke to the master of the eunuchs, "...that he should bring certain of the children is Israel," (Dan. 1:3). Daniel was referred to three times as one of the captives from Judah. Twice in Daniel they were referred to as Jews.

Daniel recognized only one Israel;

> "...to the men of Judah, and to the inhabitants of Jerusalem, and unto all Israel, that are near, and that are far off, through all the countries..." (Daniel 9:7)

Daniel knew and prophesied that even though the Jews would be scattered throughout many nations, they would be re-gathered in the latter days and make a 7-year pact with the Antichrist and go through the Tribulation. Daniel uses the term Israel four times and the term Judah seven times of the same people.

In furthering the point of Israel being one people, we have in Hosea before the destruction of either kingdom the term Israel is used 44 times and Judah 15 times. The ten tribes were to be wanderers among the nations as was Judah.

> "My god will cast them away, because they did not hearken unto him: and they shall be wanderers among the nations." (Hosea 9:17)

Hosea continued to prophecy after Israel's captivity. Amos and Micah prophesied to both kingdoms. There was not one prophet that prophesied in Israel that was exclusive to Israel and God dealt with Judah as being representative of all Israel. This was due to the fact that David's Kingdom was in Jerusalem. The ten tribes were rebellious and would not continue to participate with Judah which had the covenants and promises. In God's eyes there was Israel and Judah which was and is Israel, just as American's speak of the north and south as it were, when it was so since the Civil War.

After the northern tribes were taken to Assyria, the kingdom of Judah was referred to as Israel.

> *"...all Israel that were present went out to the cities of Judah,"* (2 Chronicles 31:1)

> *"...the children of Israel brought in abundance the first fruits..."* (2 Chronicles 31:5)

> *"and concerning the children of Israel and Judah, that dwelt in the cities of Judah,..."* (2 Chronicles 31:5)

> *"and when Hezekiah and the princes came and saw the heaps, they blessed the Lord, and his people Israel."* (2 Chronicles 31:8)

> *"...which the Levites that kept the doors had gathered of the hand of Manasseh and Ephraim, and all the remnant of Israel, and all of Judah and Benjamin;..."* (2 Chronicles 34:9)

> *"and Josiah took away all the abominations out of all the countries that pertained to the children of Israel, and made all that were present in Israel to serve,..."* (2 Chronicles 34:33)

> *All of Israel was decreed to return home from Babylon. "Who is there among you of all his people?"* (Ezra 1:3)

Cyrus, King of Persia, was charged by God to build the house of the Lord in Jerusalem, and he asked that all God's people get up to Jerusalem and build it.

Those who went out from the captivity in Babylon had come back to Jerusalem and Judah who wanted to.

"The number of the men of the people of Israel:" (Ezra 2:2)

The ones that were numbered and returned to Jerusalem,

"...dwelt in their cities, and all Israel in their cities." (Ezra 2:70)

The point here is that Jews and Israel are the same. There is no special significance to the term Israel, when used in apposition[40] to or in contrast with other names. In no instance would you find two parts of the same nation are two different kinds of people. Examples:

1 – Israel used in apposition to Reuban, God, and the half tribe of Manasseh (Joshua 22: 11-34).

"And the children of Israel sent unto the children of Reuban, and to the children of God, and to the half tribe of Manasseh," (Joshua 22:13)

A **second** example would be Israel is used in apposition to Benjamin.

"But the children of Benjamin gathered themselves together out of the cities unto Gibeah, to go out to battle against the children of Israel." (Judges 20:14)

"And the children of Israel repented them for Benjamin their brother, and said, there is one tribe cut off from Israel this day." (Judges 21:6)

Thus, naturally a third would be that Israel is used in apposition to Judah when David was king over Israel, from the tribe of Judah.

"But all Israel and Judah loved David, because he went out and came in before them" (1 Sam 18:16)

From here in Jewish history Judah would be in ascendance because of David being chosen as ruler of the now ruling tribe.

"The scepter shall not depart from Judah, nor a law-given from between his feet," (Genesis 49:10a)

Now from here one it would be made known that the Messiah would come through this tribe (Judah) because it was to be the eternal head over all the other tribes according to God's program.

"For Judah prevailed above his brethren, and of him came the chief ruler;" (1 Chronicles 5:2)

"Therefore the Lord himself shall give you a sign; Behold, a virgin shall conceive, and bear a son, and shall call his name Immanuel." (Isaiah 7:14)

Jesus Christ will be king of Israel and king of the world as is prophesied. He is to be called wonderful, Counsellor, the mighty God, the everlasting Father, the Prince of Peace.

"For unto us a child is born, unto us a son is given: and the government shall be upon his shoulder: and his name shall be called Wonderful, Counseller, The mighty God, The everlasting Father, The Prince of Peace. (Isaiah 9:6)

"Of the increase of his government and peace there shall be no end, upon the throne of David, and upon his kingdom, to order it, and to establish it with judgment and with justice from henceforth even forever." (Isaiah 9:7)

"For it is evident that our Lord sprang out of Juda;" (Hebrews 7:14)

"And one of the elders saith unto me, weep not: behold, the lion of the tribe of Juda, the root of David, hath prevailed..." (Revelation 5:5)

In the books of Kings and Chronicles there are numerous records of God cutting off many kings because of their lives of excessive sin. Finally after hundreds of years of this living in extreme sin God found it necessary to cut off both the houses of Israel.

"In the ninth year of Hoshea the king of Assyria...carried Israel away into Assyria,...

For so it was, that the children of Israel had sinned against the Lord their God," (2 King 17: 6.7)

"And the Lord said, I will remove Judah also out of my sight, as I have removed Israel." (2 Kings 23:27)

We do not find the throne of David and won't until the Millennial Kingdom, and that is not the fault of the creator, but as we see, God will not bless a sinful people who bring on the curses of God. All twelve tribes of Israel were guilty of sin and turning away from God and were sorely punished. England and America have been just as guilty of sinning against God just as all the Jewish tribes. God would not bless American and Great Britain for disobedience and rebellion, for which

Israel was punished for. It only goes to show, therefore, that the throne of David is not the British throne.

> *"For the children of Israel shall abide many days without a king, and without a prince, and without a sacrifice,…Afterward shall the children of Israel return and seek the Lord their God, and David their king:"* (Hosea 3:4, 5)

The throne of David will again be occupied at the 2nd coming of Christ, in the kingdom.

> *"After this I will return, and will build again the Tabernacle of David, which is fallen down."* (Acts 15:16)

It has been fallen down since the time of the Babylonian captivity. Jehoiachin, the son of Jehoiakim, was king for three months and ten days and the Israelites, unable to put up resistance against Nebuchadnezzar surrendered. He was then the last legitimate king to sit on David's throne in Judah, and there has been no one in line to rule there up to now. There could not have been any succession of an Israelite king or queen from then to the present queen of England. There will not be a legal heir to David's throne until the coming of the Messiah, the Lord Jesus Christ.

As stated before, the throne of David will be re-established, according to Acts 15:15, 16, after the Gentiles are completed in being called out to Christ as a people of God. The Lord will raise up the Tabernacle of David;

> *"and I will plant them upon their land, and they shall no more be pulled up out of their land which I have given them,…"* (Amos 9:15)

This is not the throne which is built up and kept up by the kings of England. Christ Jesus will build it himself.

> *"And in mercy shall he to the throne be established: and he shall sit upon it in truth in the tabernacle of David, judging, and seeking judgment, and lasting righteousness."* (Isaiah 16:5)

> *"... and the Lord God shall give unto him the throne of his father David:"* (Luke 1:32).

David's throne will be restored to Judah, not to another tribe of Israel, or to Anglo-Saxons, never Israel's descendants but descended from Japheth.

> *"that they may possess the remnant of Edom, and of all the heathen, which are called by my name, saith the Lord that doeth this."* (Amos 9:12)

No Gentile city, either in Great Britain or in the United States will be the capitol of the restored kingdom of God. It will not be London, Washington, New York City, or any other heathen city. Jerusalem shall be the capitol city and the center of the restored earth.

> *"And many people shall go and say, come ye, and let us go up to the mountain of the Lord, to the house of the God of Jacob;...for out of Zion shall go forth the law, and the word of the Lord from Jerusalem."* (Isaiah 2:3).

> *"At that time they shall call Jerusalem the throne of the Lord; and all nations shall be gathered unto it,"* (Jeremiah 3:17).

There is no hint of Judah being cut off in the scriptures from the promises and the covenants. In the Israel to come there will be a Judah included enjoying the covenants and promises with the rest of the tribes. There is not contained one Scripture that alludes to changing the capital of Israel to London. Also it is true that there is not one Scripture that changes the bestowing of the promises and covenants from Israel to London, England or a people other than the people of David or Judah or to any other particular people that is minus the tribe of Judah.

Nowhere is it stated in the Bible that Israel would be promised or given any other land other than the Divinely given land of Canaan. This was included in God's covenant to Abraham.

> *"For all the land which thou seest, to thee will I give it, and to thy seed forever."* (Genesis 13:15)

> *"In the same day the Lord made a covenant with Abram, saying, unto they seed have I given this land, from the river of Egypt unto the great river, the river Euphrates:"* (Genesis 15:18)

> *"And I will give unto thee, and to thy seed after thee, the land wherein thou art a stranger, all the land of Canaan,"* (Genesis 17:8)

This land that God promised to Abraham, Isaac, and Jacob, is in the original and only Promised land that all twelve re-gathered tribes of Israel will make an eternal nation under the Lord Jesus Christ.

> *"And there shall be an highway for the remnant of his people, which shall be left, from*

> *Assyria; like it was to Israel in the day that he came up out of the land of Egypt."* (Isaiah 11:16)

> *But, the Lord liveth, that brought up the children of Israel from the land of the north, and from all the lands whither he had driven them: and I will bring them again into their land that I gave unto their fathers."* (Jeremiah 16:15)

> *"That they may walk in my statutes, and keep mine ordinances, and do them: and they shall be my people, and I will be their God."* (Ezekiel 11:20)

Just to interject between the proofs against British – Israelism, the Anglo-Israelist needs to answer some important questions. Number one is proving that the ten tribes were actually once lost. If they were, how do they know? Second, prove now that they have found the lost tribes of Israel. If they have, what is the means by which they have identified them? Third, these groups must prove that the British and Americans are the people of these lost tribes. If not by their descent which has proven to be lacking, then how? Fourth, they must without leaving any doubts prove that England is Ephraim and the United States is Manasseh. Over all these years the Anglo-Israelists have failed in this task. Fifth, they must prove that the ten tribes alone make up the house of Israel, in which there are no Jews.

The Lord shall:

> *"...assemble the outcasts of Israel, and gather together the dispersed of Judah from the four corners of the earth."* (Isaiah 12:12)

Both houses of Israel and Judah were to be gathered and assembled as the outcasts of Israel and the dispersed of Judah as the victor over their enemies. This first dispersion was to be in two parts, one into Assyria and one into Babylon. Under Ezra and Nehemiah the first re-gathering took place. There will be a second re-gathering which proves that some from all 10 tribes were gathered the first time under Ezra and Nehemiah. It wasn't only some from Judah above that returned to Jerusalem.

We know that the second complete expulsion of the Jews from their land was when Jerusalem was destroyed in 70 A.D. and was completed by 130 A.D. All Israel will be re-gathered at the second coming of Christ and include all Jews of all twelve tribes.

> *"Immediately after the tribulation of those days...and then shall all the tribes of the earth mourn, and they shall see the son of man...and they shall gather together his elect..."* (Matthew 24: 29-31)

If there are any lost tribes in America or Britain, they would be required to relocate in Palestine, but that is against the teachings of Anglo-Israelism. All tribes, including Judah, were dispersed among the nations, so all must be re-gathered for a second time the same as the first time under Ezra and Nehemiah.

The house of Israel and the house of Judah will become one nation in the same land, the land promised to Abraham, Isaac, and Jacob, after the second re-gathering after the Tribulation.

> *"And I will make them one nation in the land upon the mountains of Israel;"* (Ezekiel 37:22)

The Lord Jesus Christ will be their Messiah forever.

> *"And the heathen shall know that I the Lord do sanctify Israel, when my sanctuary shall be in the midst of them for evermore."* (Ezekiel 37:28)

When David is resurrected in the Millennium, he will be king to reign over both united houses of Israel as in time past.

> *"But they shall serve the Lord their God and David their king, whom I will raise up unto them"* (Jeremiah 30:9)

In the future, the twelve apostles will be on twelve thrones judging the twelve tribes of Israel, under their king David and under their Messiah, the Lord Jesus Christ.

> *"...ye also shall sit upon twelve thrones, judging the twelve tribes of Israel."* (Matthew 19:28)

This means that at this time, when they are under the twelve judges, that all of the tribes of Israel will be present together in Israel. We cannot have assurance the Anglo-Saxon people of England and America will be there, for they will not ever go out of their own countries as a re-gathered people in Palestine.

This gathering of the twelve tribes of Israel will be in the latter days.

> *"When thou art in Tribulation,...even in the latter days,...he will not forsake thee,...nor forget the covenant of thy fathers..."* (Deuteronomy 4:30, 31)

They will then go through the tribulation, called the time of Jacob's Trouble, Daniel's 70th week, then they are both to be saved out of it, then ruled by King David and the Lord Jesus Christ.

God promises to gather all the families, all the tribes of Israel, and not just Judah only.

> *"At the same time, saith the Lord, will I be the God of all the families of Israel, and they shall be my people."* (Jeremiah 31:1)

> *"...He that scattered Israel will gather him, and keep him, as a shepherd doth his flock. Therefore, they shall come and sing in the height of Zion,"* (Jeremiah 31:10b, 12a)

A new covenant will be instituted by God with both houses of Israel.

> *"Behold, the days come, saith the Lord, that I will make a new covenant with the house of Israel, and with the house of Judah:"* (Jeremiah 31:31)

Another problem with the Anglo-Israelism is this: they cut off Judah from all the everlasting covenants and promises made to them by God, claiming that these are fulfilled by Anglo-Saxons. They also claim, falsely, that Israel of the prophets has no tribe of Judah.

After the return of the 12 tribes of Israel, there will be a repopulating of the land and property will be increased, all brought on by the blessings of Christ Jesus.

> *"Men shall buy fields for money, and subscribe evidences, and seal them, and take witnesses in the land of Benjamin, and in the places about Jerusalem, and in the cities of Judah, and in the cities of the mountains, and in*

110

the cities of the valley, and in the cities of the south:" (Jeremiah 32:44)

This will be a great rebuilding and it is not inclusive of the cities of London, in England, nor the cities in America such as Washington.

The house of Judah was to be saved and Jerusalem would dwell in safety in the Kingdom of Jesus Christ. There is nothing said about an Israel as being a separate people somewhere in a land northwest who will never be moved to Palestine.

> *"In those days shall Judah be saved, and Jerusalem shall dwell safely: and this is the name wherewith she shall be called, the Lord our righteousness.* (Jeremiah 33:16)

All twelve tribes of Israel, including the Levites, will be planted back in their own land, promised to them by the Lord. Until then the Prophesies of the Kingdom of Israel cannot be fulfilled.

> *"And I will bring again the captivity of my people of Israel, and they shall build the waste cities, and inhabit them; ...and I will plant them upon their land, and they shall no more be pulled out of their land..."* (Amos 9:14a, 15a)

The curses and punishment God put upon Israel for their sin were to be for all twelve tribes alike.

> *"The land also shall be left of them, and shall enjoy her Sabbaths,...and they shall accept of the punishment of their iniquity:"* (Leviticus 26:43)

> *"And thy life shall hang in doubt before thee; and thou shalt fear day and night,"* (Deut. 28:66)

111

All of the tribes of Israel are continuing under these punishments even today as they were scattered, and still some remain scattered throughout the nations. The British Isles and the United States of America, not being scattered as such, cannot have fulfilled nor cannot now be fulfilling God's predictions; not like the Jews of the world.

Nowhere in the Bible at any time is there a reference to a people called Israel being distinct from Jews in the New Testament. For the terms "Jews" and "Israel" are used interchangeably in the entire New Testament, also after the captivity of the ten tribes in 2 Kings 17. The term "Jew" is used fifty-three times is Ester. After the ten-tribe kingdom of Israel was destroyed in 749 B.C, Judah and other of the ten tribes living in Israel represented all Israel. The term "Jew" is equivalent to "Israelite" and is so used in Scripture. One cannot be separated from the other. "Jew" is used ninety-one times in the Old Testament, and two hundred and two times in the New Testament. They are terms describing the same class of people. One cannot use Jew only of Judah.

> "Now in Sushan the palace there was a certain Jew, whose name was Mordecai,...a Benjamite;" (Ester 2:5)

> But Paul said, I am a man which am a Jew of Tarsus, a city of Cilicia," (Acts 21:3 9)

> "Circumcised the eighth day, of the stock of Israel, of the tribe of Benjamin,...(Philippians 3:5)

It is the Jews and Gentiles that are shown to be distinct groups in the Bible.

> *"...of the Jew first, and also of the Gentiles;"* (Romans 2:9)

> *"No, in no wise: for we have before proved both Jews and Gentiles that they are all under sin;"* (Romans 3:9)

> *"Even us, when he hath called, not of the Jews only, but also of the Gentiles?"* (Romans 9:24)

> *"Give none offense, neither to the Jews, nor to the Gentiles, nor to the church of God."* (1 Corinthians 10:32)

> *"For by one spirit are we all baptized into one body, whether we be Jews or Gentiles,"* (1 Corinthians 12:13)

All tribes are still Jews and Israelites, even today.

> *"Unto which promises our twelve tribes, instantly serving God day and night, hope to come."* (Acts 26:7)

> *"And I heard the number of them which were sealed: and there were sealed an hundred and forty and four thousand of all the tribes of the children of Israel."* (Revelation 7:4)

> *"And had a wall great and high,...thereon, which are the names of the twelve tribes of the children of Israel."* (Revelation 21:12)

The house of Israel and the house of Judah are to return from the nations in the last days and are to be blessed under the Lord.

> *"In those days the house of Judah shall walk with the house of Israel,"* (Jeremiah 3:18a)

113

A thorough study of the words "Jew and "Israel" both in the Old and New Testaments will yield that the Anglo-Saxon or British-Israel theory of driving a distinction between the two, and on top of that creating an Anglo-Saxon ten-tribe theory to be false.

The 2520-year long theory, claimed that Israel would be absent from world leadership from 721 B.C. to 1800 A.D., when England's greatness had begun. It was further claimed that Israel's removal fulfilled the seven times punishment of Leviticus 26, which is unscriptural. The fact that England came into world power at that time proves nothing in regards to her identity as being the ten lost tribes.

In the book of Psalms, the term "Jews" is found only once. The term "Israel" is found sixty-two times and "Judah" is found ten times pertaining to the same people. There are no northern and southern kingdoms referred to at all. Israel and Judah, when mentioned, refer to the same people, the descendants of Abraham, Isaac, and Jacob.

British-Israelism, or Anglo-Israelism is then shown to not be the migration point for the ten tribes of Israel. When the ten tribes split from Judah, those who were godly and remained true to King David were constantly migrating into the kingdom of Judah.

> "But as for the children of Israel which dwelt in the cities of Judah, Rehoboam reigned over them." (1 Kings 12:17)

> "And in Jerusalem dwelt of the children of Judah,...and of the children of Ephraim and Manasseh." (1 Chronicles 9:3)

> *"Speak unto Rehoboam the son of Solomon, king of Judah, and to all Israel in Judah, and Benjamin,"* (2 Chronicles 11:3)

> *"And he gathered all Judah and Benjamin, and the strangers with them out of Ephraim and Manasseh, and out of Simeon: for they fell to him out of Israel in abundance,"* (2 Chronicles 15:9)

> *"And concerning the children of Israel and Judah, that dwelt in the cities of Judah,"* (2 Chronicles 31:6a)

It is obvious then that there were substantial numbers of Israelites that were not of Judah and Benjamin always present in Jerusalem and in Judah. There was such a troubling amount leaving the north that King Basha, King of Israel," built Ramah, to the intent that he might let none go out or come in to Asa, king of Judah." (2 Chronicles 16:1). There was a decrease in the Kingdom of Israel, (supposed to be Anglo-Saxons) and such an increase in Judah which was plain to see. The godly ones of Israel's ten northern tribes were leaving the idolatrous northern kingdom of Israel. Israel lost large numbers in battles until they were no match for the Syrians.

> *"...and the children of Israel pitched before them like two little flocks of kids; but the Syrians filled the country."* (1 Kings 20:27)

The so-called ten tribes were decimated and needed the Lord to deliver them this time from the Syrians. But Israel was hardening their heart against the Lord because of their extreme sin cast them in captivity in 721 B.C. Ninety years after the Assyrian deportation, Second Chronicles 35:18 records Israel observing the Passover with Judah.

115

Many Israelites had fled the northern Kingdom from the Assyrians and many more fled to Judah after the Assyrians broke up and destroyed Israel; 2 Chronicles 15:9 shows the resettlement before the deportation.

> *"And there was one Anna, a prophetess,...of the Tribe of Aser (Asher)."* (Luke 2:36)

Anna, from the New Testament was of the tribe of Asher, one of the supposed ten lost tribes. Many were never heard from again after being carried off into Assyria. Those were probably put in groups to settle among other Assyrians and any semblance of Jewishness having disappeared.

There is evidence in scripture and elsewhere to prove that the ten tribes were never lost, but rejoined with Judah in the south. Also, when Babylon conquered the southern kingdom, the people would have sought out the Israelites in Assyria and joined with them. In the return from Babylon, which was Persia by then, there was no limit on returnees as being entirely from the tribe of Judah.[41]

Judah Carried Away

> *"And I said after she had done all these things turn thou unto me. But she returned not. And her treacherous sister Judah saw it."* (Jeremiah 3:7)

> *"...yet her treacherous sister Judah feared not, but went and played the harlot also..."* (Jeremiah 3:8b)

"And yet for all this her treacherous sister Judah hath not turned unto me with her whole heart," (Jeremiah 3:10)

"And the Lord said unto me, the backsliding Israel hath justified herself more than treacherous Judah." (Jeremiah 3:11)

God has put the southern kingdom of Judah on alert and on a very short leash.

"Now in the fourteenth year of King Hezekiah did Sennacherib King of Assyria come up against all the fenced cities of Judah, and took them." (2 Kings 18:13)

This was in 704 B.C. Hezekiah bought off the Assyrians and they withdrew from Judah. Hezekiah tried to hold off the Assyrians and ended up paying tribute to them. This was the first invasion of Judah by Sennacherib.

Hearing that Assyrian territories were being invaded, the king of Assyria sent his force against Jerusalem.

Jerusalem Threatened

The Assyrians presented a fearsome and bloody promise to Hezekiah demanding payment or suffer sure destruction. On top of that, Judah was to surrender the kingdom and to submit all Israelites to be carried off to Assyria. Tartan, Rabsaris and Rab-Shakeh greeted Judah's representatives with vile insults and blasphemies. They are brainwashing the Jews and trying to intimidate them.

So the servants of Hezekiah bring the report to Hezekiah that Judah is too weak to withstand Assyria's verbal or military attacks. The distress and turmoil of Hezekiah causes him to go to the house of God, and for the others to seek out the prophet Isaiah. It is Isaiah that gives them a prophecy.

> *"Behold, I will send a blast upon him, and he shall hear a rumour, and shall return to his own land; and I will cause him to fall by the sword in his own land.* (2 Kings 19:7)

> *"And it came to pass that night, that the angel of the Lord went out, and smote in the camp of the Assyrians an hundred fourscore and five thousand:* (2 Kings 19:35)

> *"And it came to pass, as he (Sennacherib) was worshipping in the house of Nisroch his god, that Adrammelech and Sharezer his sons smoke him with the sword:"* (2 Kings 19:37)

When the northern kingdom had been taken into captivity for their sins, God then and there warned Judah that the same fate awaited them.

> *"Also Judah kept not the commandments of the Lord their God, but walked in the statutes of Israel which they made."* (2 Kings 17:19)

There were eight kings of Judah from the time of the destruction of the northern kingdom until the Babylonian Captivity. This was a period of around 135 years and Hezekiah, Manasseh, Amon, Josiah, Johoahaz, Jehoiakim, Jehoiachin, and Zedekiah were the final eight kings.

After the 10 tribes were in captivity Judah sank deeper into sin and then they were finally destroyed. It took over one hundred more years because God showed mercy on Judah for the good kings, relatively speaking, Hezekiah and Josiah.

But Judah as a whole was in big trouble.

"For her wound is incurable; for it is come unto Judah; he is come unto the gate of my people, even to Jerusalem." (Micah 1:9)

Judah's sin and apostasy had become so great it became incurable. The Hebrew for incurable is *"anas(h)"*, which means to be sick, in poor health, to be in a weakened state that is leading to death. This is a peek on Judah's condition inside Jerusalem after 701 B.C. It contained incurably wicked Jews (Jer. 17:9) preying on the weaker and infirm poorer Jews.

So, then, the desperately and incurable wicked were thrown together with the desperately sick and ill, the total state of which God would only know the extent of. The implication is that these desperate groups were so woeful in their wickedness and illness as to be unaware how desperate they actually were.

For the sins of Judah; their idolatry, and their apostasy, they were heading for judgment from God. Although God has already judged Israel and is about to judge Judah, he loves the souls of sinners and will return the members of the remnant that repent and turn to God. For all the darkness and doom that is descending on the split kingdom, there is redemption on their horizon.

"Who is a God like unto thee, that pardoneth iniquity and passeth by the transgression of the remnant of his heritage? He retaineth not his anger forever, because he delighted in mercy." (Micah 7:18)

Many, many times the nation of Israel has seen the actions towards them as a God like none other, a God who has no equal. They learned that

He is the living God, the Creator of heaven and earth and all that is in it. However, they worshipped the creature rather than the Creator. They were burdened with the iniquity of idols in the form of covetousness, materialism; for all the things the soul gives itself to is god. All the things that are likened unto God makes him equal to those things.

So for Judah, idolatry ranked number one, for their covetousness and materialism filled their hearts so much so that they turned their backs to God. All the pleasures that money can bring became their god. The gods they were worshipping were small, insignificant gods. They had contemptable gods, ugly gods, evil gods.

The Israelites flaunted these terrible gods in God's face which is blasphemous. God is holy and God gets His wrath up and directed at sin. Idol worship and sinning leads to a holy God's wrath and then judgment.

> *"...because they have despised the law of the Lord, and have not kept his commandments, and their lies caused them to err,...But I will send a fire upon Judah, and it shall devour the palaces of Jerusalem."* (Amos 2:4, 5)

God judged Judah for their idolatry, despising God's law, not keeping His commandments, and walking in the sinful ways and lies like their fathers.

In the 135 years from Assyrian exile until the Babylonian captivity there were two good kings out of the last eight. Those two good kings were King Hezekiah and King Josiah. The one bad king was very bad and God allowed the Babylonians captivity to be carried out due to his excessive sins.

Hezekiah

Hezekiah ruled over Judah from 726 to 687 B.C. for 29 years. He was very aggressive in instituting great reforms and destroyed idol worship everywhere in Judah.

> *"He removed the high places, and broke the images, and cut down the groves,"* (2 Kings 18:4)

In the sixth year of Hezekiah's reign in Judah, the king of Assyria carried off the ten tribes of Israel into captivity. Then five years later Sennacherib, king of Assyria, took all the outlying fenced cities of Judah up to the gates of Jerusalem. Assyrian king Sennacherib laid siege on Jerusalem in 701 B.C.

Proverbs 25:1 states that the proverbs of Solomon were copied out by the men of Hezekiah. King Ahaz, Hezekiah's father erected altars to false gods in every section of Jerusalem. In every city of Judah:

> *"...he made high places to burn incense unto other gods, and provoked to anger the Lord."* (2 Chron. 28:25)

Good King Hezekiah came along and:

> *"He removed the high places, and brake the images, and cut down the groves, and broke in pieces the brazen serpent that Moses had made:"* (2 Kings 18:4)

Next, Hezekiah had to confront the Syrian invasion mentioned before. That account of Hezekiah's preparations and resistance is found in 2 Chronicles 32:1-10. But the Syrians threatened and intimidated the Hebrews to despair until Hezekiah along with Isaiah both prayed and cried out to the Lord. The Lord then killed all the Syrian soldiers, so Sennacherib returned home to his fate.

Hezekiah then fell ill with a sickness which would have led to death. Hezekiah then prayed unto God, reminding Him of his obedience and his perfect heart towards God. God answered the king's prayers by adding to his life fifteen years.

King Hezekiah got in trouble with pride in his heart which lifted him up because of riches. Gold had blessed him with great wealth: silver and gold, great stores of spices, and precious ointment, much armor, and many more treasures of his. He had accumulated a lot of things, precious and valuable things. This drew the attention of the Babylonians and the kind, and in great pride, showed to them all his riches. He put it all on display for the so-called friendly Babylonians. That prompted Isaiah to approach Hezekiah and rebuke him sharply for the foolishness he had done. Isaiah prophesied that everything of any value would be taken by the Babylonians. Sadly, this also included the king's sons to be taken and would become eunuchs in the Babylonian palace.

Manasseh

Hezekiah died and was buried in the ascent of the sepulchers of the sons of David. He was honored by all Judah and all the inhabitants of Jerusalem. His son Manasseh, then started the most evil reign ever in Judah. According to Thiele's charts Manasseh reigned for 10 years, from 697-687 B.C. At the age of 22 he ruled Judah as sole king from 687-643 B.C. for a total of 55 years. This was the longest reign of any king of Israel or Judah.

It is known in Israelite records as the great age of reaction, and there seems to have been no other time in her whole history when Judah was guilty of so great and complicated an apostasy.[42]

That is putting it mildly, for God brought final punishment and captivity upon Judah solely for the sinning in excess by Manasseh. The name Manasseh was synonymous with evil and there is no other comparison when it comes to him.

> *"And he did that which was evil in the sight of the Lord, after the abominations of the heathen, whom the Lord cast out before the children of Israel."* (2 Kings 21:2)

According to 2 Kings 21:3-7, to enumerate, he rebuilt the high places of Baal worship, he built altars to Baal also, he made groves of immorality, worshipped every god that was known at the time, and served them. He built heathen, sacrilegious altars in the Temple of God. He built altars for each and every one of the pagan gods in the two courts of the house of God. Manasseh initiated an idolatry unsurpassed in Judah, offered human sacrifices, including his own son, encouraged sorcery and witchcraft. The reward for such behavior is the loss of children and widowhood (Isaiah 47:9). These are judgments that God will bring upon the Empire of Babylon, which were applied during the reign of Manasseh and because of it.

> *"And I will come near to you to judgment:"* (Mal. 3:5)

Manasseh brought much wickedness in the sight of the Lord, and this provoked the Lord very much. God commanded the Israelites to observe God's law, but they refused to listen and the king was implicated in this.

"And Manasseh seduced them to do more evil than did the nations..." (2 Kings 21:9)

Manasseh by being the promoter of evil turned Judah completely spiritually deaf to God. This stubbornness of evil, total witchcraft, sparked the anger of God towards Judah.

"Because Manasseh king of Judah hath done these abominations,...Behold, I am bringing such evil upon Jerusalem and Judah,... And I will forsake the remnant of mine inheritance, and deliver them into the hand of their enemies;" (2 Kings 2:11)

It is chilling how Judah has so provoked the Lord, that now there will be no saving Judah from defeat and captivity. This is now 697.B.C. He had made Judah and the inhabitants of Jerusalem to become worse than the heathens who were destroyed before the Israelites inhabited Canaan. So, in 681 B.C., the Assyrians took and bound King Manasseh off to Babylon. Manasseh then appealed to God while locked up and the Lord in his mercy forgave and restored him.

"...and heard his supplication, and brought him again to Jerusalem into his kingdom. The Manasseh knew that the Lord he was God." (2 Chron. 33:13)

However, the die was cast and the fate of Judah was in God's hands.

Josiah

In 634 B.C. Josiah was eight years old when he started to reign in Judah. He reigned for thirty-one years, until 609 B.C., and was the very last good king which probably delayed the Babylonian captivity for another twenty-five years.

Josiah was next to the youngest king in Israel. He was born to and brought up by the wicked king Amon, the son of Manasseh. He became one of the most faithful servants of almighty God. Josiah was a fulfillment of Ezekiel 18, which says that a son of an evil father need not turn out evil.

> "When the son hath done that which is lawful and right, and hath kept all my statutes, and hath done them, he shall surely live." (Ezekiel 18:19)

Besides doing what was right in the sight of God, he did not deviate in all the ways of David the king. Josiah was the only king of whom this could be said. (2 King 22:2)

There were many religious changes that occurred under Josiah besides reversing the evil, pagan ways of Manasseh and Amon. In his eighteenth year of rule he ordered the renovation and repair of the temple, which had been desecrated in the last 60 years. The high priest at the time, Hilkiah, found the Book of the Law and gave it to the scribe, Shaphan. The wicked kings may have put away the original Pentateuch which was now uncovered. The king ordered three faithful servants to enquire of the lord as to what they should do.

They went to Huldah, the prophetess, and she prophesied about its content. The evil forecast for Judah was to come, but not in his day due to the tenderness and humility of Josiah before the Lord. God promised to bring evil upon the land and the inhabitants of Judah and Jerusalem.

The wrath that God brings against the land and sinful people will not be quenched until all is destroyed. Because Josiah wept and repented for Judah, God would make sure the King would die in peace and in the grace of God. God promised Josiah that he would not see with his own eyes the desolation coming to Judah. Judah would be destroyed for forsaking God and burning incense in worship to heathen gods.

Josiah then embarked on ending the pagan, ritualistic Israelite religious practices and the astral cults that had integrated into Jewish religions in the 8th century B.C. Josiah made a solemn covenant with the Lord. He stood in the reserved place in the temple for the king (2 Chron. 34:31) by one of the pillars, and made the covenant to keep the law, and to make Israel to keep His commandments, His testimonies, and His statutes, with all their hearts.

Josiah cleansed Judah of all idols and idol worship. He destroyed all the human sacrifice altars and all the high places of idol worship. Images of pagan deities and all pagan sources of false worship were destroyed throughout the land of Israel and Jerusalem.

He then commanded the people to keep a Passover unto the Lord. Somehow there was not a Passover in the days of the Kings of Israel nor the Kings of Judah.

"Notwithstanding the Lord turned not from the fierceness of his great wrath, wherewith his anger was kindled against Judah, because of all the provocations that Manasseh had provoked with withal." (2 Kings 23:26)

For the next 23 years, after King Josiah died, Judah was led down a dark path of utter destruction and finally captivity.

The Fall

Four prophets figure prominently during the full collapse of Judah and Jerusalem. Zephaniah is found in the reign of Josiah and was the contemporary of a young prophet Jeremiah. Nahum had prophesied before the fall of Nineveh around 612 B.C. Habakkuk was active in the reign of Jehoiakim from 609-598 B.C. He saw the rise of the empire Babylon and the danger it presented to Judah.

"For, lo, I raise up the Chaldeans,...they shall come all for violence:..." (Hab. 1:6, 9)

He also warned his people that the Babylonians were only there to destroy Judah plus:

"...and they shall gather the captivity as the sand." (V9)

The prophet Ezekiel was in his ministry as of the fifth year of Jehoiachin's captivity in 593 B.C. and continued in that office even after the captivity of 586 B.C.

"In the five and twentieth year of our captivity...in the fourteenth year after that that city was smitten,..." (Ezekiel 40:1)

These were not the only prophets concerned or alive during this time of Judah's trouble. Joel and Jeremiah were also present. In fact, Jeremiah saw that the reforms of King Josiah would not be enough to pull Judah out of her sin and apostasy for long.

> *"They have healed also the hurt of the daughter of my people slightly, saying peace, peace; when there is no peace"* (Jeremiah 6:14)

Jeremiah pleaded with the people to stand and walk in the Lord's ways and to ask for the old paths and walk in the good way, but they rejected that. They were to be watchmen and to respond to the sound of the trumpet, but they would not hear. The people only continued to burn incense and offer burnt offerings to every strange god.

The nation had false prophets which spoke falsely and misled the people (Jer. 5:31). These were the evil among them which set them up for blatant sin and rejection of God, (Jeremiah 5: 26, 27). The religious leaders did not discourage the people in their worldly pursuits or blasphemies.

> *"What have I done? Every one turned to his course, as the horse rusheth into the battle."* (Jer. 8:6)

Their burnt sacrifices and offerings were no longer pleasing to God, for they were only external, cultic expressions to serve a spiritually dead heart. They had become busy in their religion, and engaged in disobedience to the heart of God.

> *"O Jerusalem, wash thine heart from wickedness, that thou mayest be saved."* (Jeremiah 4:14)

> *Circumcise therefore the foreskin of your heart, and be no more stiffnecked."* (Deuteronomy 10:16)

Judah became a vassel entity of Egypt. They took Jehoahaz away in captivity to Egypt. Jehoiakim, the brother of Jehoahaz was weak and Egypt put a heavy tribute on Judah.

> *"He exacted the silver and the gold of the people of the land,...to give it unto Pharoah-nechoh."* (2 Kings 23:35)

These last four kings of Judah were a total disaster. Instead of leading the people into worship of the true God and upholding His will and His law, they did the exact opposite. God wants obedience from His people. Obedience to God will preserve the covenant with him and enable God to rule over his people. But the people would not repent, nor break up their fallow ground, or even circumcise their hearts to stand pure before their God.

God is raising up a foe against the Israelites far worse than the Egyptians or the Assyrians. These are the Babylonians and God says:

> *"Blow ye the trumpet in the land:...for I will bring evil from the north,...he is gone forth from his place to make thy land desolate; for the fierce anger of the Lord is not turned back from us."* (Jeremiah 4:5-8)

King Jehoiakim was made king in 609 B.C. In 605 B.C. Nebuchadnezzar, then a prince, defeated the Egyptians at Carchemish on the Euphrates which dealt such a blow that Egypt was unable to recover. Jehoiakim was Nebuchadnezzar's servant for three years, and then he rebelled against the

Chaldees. This is when the Lord sent against Jehoiakim raiding bands of Chaldees, Syrians, Moabites, and Ammonites. This was the result of the sins of Manasseh (2 King 24:3).

Jehoiachin reigned next after Jehoiakim. Babylon then besieged Jerusalem. The king surrendered to the king of Babylon along with his royal family, officers of the court, and the top tiers of the population were deported to Babylon. This was in the 8th year of the reign of Nebuchadrezzar, in 597 B.C. and totaled 3,023 deportees. The Babylonian king took to Babylon the survivors of the siege, able-bodied soldiers, craftsmen and artisans. Daniel was included in the deportation to Babylon.

> *"In the eighteenth year of Nebuchadrezzar he carried away captive from Jerusalem eight hundred thirty and two persons:"* (Jeremiah 52:29).

This is the second deportation of Jews to Babylon. This happened in the year 586 B.C. This time the walls surrounding Jerusalem were demolished and the temple destroyed as the entire city lay in ruins.

> *"In the three and twentieth year of Nebuchadrezzar Nebuzaraden the captain of the guard carried away captive of the Jews seven hundred forty and five persons: all the persons were four thousand and six hundred* (Jeremiah 52:30*).*

This was the third and final deportation of the Jews of Judah and Jerusalem to be carried off in captivity to Babylon. The commonwealth of the nation of Israel was ended. There were some poor

Jews that were allowed to remain in the outlying areas, but they had no temple and no pure-line priests.

This was a minor, first Diaspora or scattering of Jews that made their way out of Israel. Jerusalem was destroyed, burnt, and emptied of prior residents. Some scattered survivors that could get away fled north to Samaria, east to Edom, and Moab, and south to Egypt.

Return from Babylon

We must remember that the number of Jews deported to Babylon was a total of 4,600, as we find in Jeremiah 52: 28-30. 2 Kings 24:14 gives a total of 10,000 which included royalty, soldiers, craftsmen and smiths. That's a difference of 5,400, which may have as a result of those that died of brutal conditions on the way to Babylon.

They were allowed to settle together as a Jewish conclave, or conclaves, free to mingle and make up some kind of community life, earning a living, engaging in trade, and some became very wealthy.

> "Thus saith the Lord of hosts, ...unto all that are carried away captives,..." (Jeremiah 29:"4)

God cared for his people, sending instructions for captivity and how to serve Him and prosper. They were to build their own dwellings, harvest vegetables and eat their own fruit. They were to marry and be fruitful as well as their sons and daughters. They were to be peaceful in their cities and pray to the Lord and not hearken to false prophets and fortune tellers.

For God knew how long they would be in captivity.

> *"For thus saith the Lord, That after seventy years be accomplished at Babylon I will visit you, and perform my good word toward you, in causing you to return to this place"* (Jeremiah 29:10)

In Daniel 9:2 Daniel knows by the book of Jeremiah that after 70 years the captivity in Babylon will be over according to God. Shortly the Jewish Captives will be given the opportunity to return to Israel. Daniel acknowledges in his prayer that it is God's mercy that this remnant of the nation of Israel has been preserved. Even though they have committed iniquity, wickedness, rebellion, disobedience, and turning a deaf ear to God's prophets. Daniel prayed for Judah, the inhabitants of Jerusalem, and unto all Israel (the 10 tribes) for they were near and others far off (scattered). Daniel confessed sin for the whole of Israel, for the state they were in, as well as his own personal sin. They were in such a state for their own sinful hearts and that through the righteousness of God, Israel may one day be righteous in the Lord.

Cyrus

Cyrus the Great established the Persian Empire and he reigned from 559-530 B.C. This reign lasted about 30 years after conquering the Median Empire, then the Lydian Empire, and finally the Babylonian Empire. He executed a model for centralized government and favored the success and profit of his subjects.

132

In the book of Ezra in chapter one, verse two, it states, "the Lord God of heaven hath given me all the kingdoms of the earth;" (Ez. 1:2). This so-called knowledge of God has stirred great controversy and wild speculation, not the least of which is stated in the Dake Bible notes. It says, this knowledge of God was given to Cyrus by his mother, the Jewish queen Esther, and by Mordecai and Nehemiah. He was brought up in Jewish training and taught about God and His word.[43] However, not to get hopes up, it is stated in Wikipedia, Cyrus the Great, was born to Cambyses I, King of Anshan, and Mandane, daughter of Astyages, King of Media, during the period of 600-599 B.C.

<u>Restoration of Israel</u>

Cyrus figured prominently in the return of the Jewish remnant to Israel and its restoration. He led Persia in an enlightened way, evidently led by Daniel to an understanding of the living, true God. Scripture does not tell us if Cyrus gave his heart to God and became a believer.

This may be a stretch to call Cyrus anything other than God's instrument in effecting a return of the Jews from captivity. Scripture states not one moral or religious virtue as the qualification of this Gentile to the title of God's anointed or Messiah.[44] Indeed no Hebrew could have praised the faith of this Persian who styled himself "the servant of Marduk." Cyrus has credited the god Marduk for calling him to Babylon and his occupation of the city. From the translation of the Cylinder of Cyrus by L. W. King, we read about this relationship between Cyrus and Marduk: "He (i.e., Marduk) sought out a righteous prince after his own heart, who he might take by the hand; Cyrus, king of Anshan, he called by his name, for empire over the whole world he proclaimed his title...Marduk the great lord, protector of his people, beheld his upright deeds and his righteous heart with joy To his city of Babylon he commanded him to go, like a friend and helper he went by his side...without contest and battle he made him enter into Babylon his city."[45]

"And Cyrus himself declares, "Marduk the great lord [inclined] the great heart of the sons of Babylon to me, and daily do I care for his worship...and the gods of Sumer and Akkad which Nabumahid had brought into Babylon, at the word of Marduk, the great lord, one and all in their own shrines did I cause to take up the habitation of their heart's delight. May all the gods whom I have brought into their own cities pray daily before Bel and Nabu for the lengthening of my days, "etc.[46]

Cyrus was no monotheist. He had a knowledge of God as we read in Ezra 1:1, but there was no heart knowledge beyond the God of Israel as being just another of the gods of Cyrus.

> *"For Jacob my servant's sake, and Israel mine elect, I have even called thee by my name: I have surnamed thee, though thou hast not known me. I girded thee, though thou has hast not known me:"* (Isaiah 45: 4, 5)

To God, Israel must need to be redeemed and freed from their captivity and settled back in their land. Cyrus just happens to be the fittest piece of the plan, to be His anointed, or Messiah, and has called by His name for the sake of His servant Jacob and Israel His chosen. For the previous 70 years the world has witnessed the emptying of the promised land of its inhabitants.

> *"That saith of Cyrus, he is my shepherd, and shall perform all my pleasure: even saying to Jerusalem, Thou shalt be built; and to the temple, Thy foundation shall be laid.*: (Isaiah 44:28)

Cyrus then is the chosen instrument to perform God's unstoppable will, to free his people from the Chaldean captivity. God has chosen Cyrus, neither because of his character or that he is given one by God, but he is there, and a sovereign choice by God. He is a tool of God and possesses no other qualification but to have the qualities of a tool. All the forces, of which one is force that converged around Cyrus, are in God's hands and may be used by him as a means of grace. We are all still upon the Potter's wheel as was Cyrus, being used by the Potter's hands. God uses all means, He reigns, for the purposes nearest His heart, in a final victory of righteousness.

> *"I form the light, and create darkness: I make peace, and create evil: I the Lord do all these things."* (Isaiah 45:7)

The Decree

> *"The Lord stirred up the spirit of Cyrus King of Persia, that he made a proclamation throughout all his kingdom, and put it also in writing,..."* (2 Chronicles 36:22)

> *"The Lord stirred up the spirit of Cyrus King of Persia, that he made a proclamation throughout all his kingdom, and put it also in writing.."* (Ezra 1:1)

135

The repeated verse from 2 Chronicles 36: 22-23, is put there by God to give hope for the future in Israel's darkest time. The historical record continues in Ezra from this point. And the important precept here is the commencement of the building of the walls and city of Jerusalem, which is covered by three kings and their decrees: Cyrus, Darius, and Artexerxes. These decrees are found to be covered in the book of Ezra. These decrees without any exception have to do with the rebuilding of the "temple, not the city."[47]

> *"Thus saith Cyrus King of Persia, all the kingdoms of the earth hath the Lord God of heaven given me; and he hath charged me to build him an house in Jerusalem, which is in Judah. Who is there among you of all his people? The Lord his God be with him, and let him go up."* (2 Chronicles 36:23).

Two things are clear here. First, Cyrus is charged, or commanded, to build a house in Jerusalem. The word for house in Hebrew, *bavith,* means Temple. The other thing is, the door was swung open for the people of God to leave Babylon to go to Jerusalem to build the temple.

Ezra 4:1 says in part, *"...the children of the captivity builded the temple unto the Lord God of Israel."*

In fact, the rebuilding of the Temple, or "house of the Lord" was suspended for a period of time so that those heathen peoples who opposed the Jews could be answered. Darius made a search for and found the original decree of Cyrus concerning,"...the house of God at Jerusalem, let the house be builded,...and let the foundations thereof be strongly laid;" (Ezra 6:3). This was the second decree, this one made by Darius that again only concerned the rebuilding of the Temple. This was in 519 B.C. as found in Ezra 5:1-17. The decree of Cyrus was back in 536 B.C. and is found in Ezra 1:1-4.

After the second letter (decree) was delivered to the Jews, work progressed and was encouraged. First was the push from Haggai found in 1:12:

> "Then Zerubabel the son of Shealtiel, and Joshua the son of Josedech, the high priest, with all the remnant of the people, obeyed the voice of the Lord their God,..." (Haggai 1:12)

> "Thus saith the Lord of hosts; If it be marvelous in the eyes of the remnant of this people in these days, should it also be marvelous in mine eyes? Saith the Lord of hosts." (Zech. 8:6)

The people were pleased with the rebuilding of God's house, and God said He was pleased too.

Returning Remnant

The first expedition out of Babylon was led by Zerubbabel who was a governor in post-Babylonian Israel. Jeshua is second-mentioned (Ezra 2:2) and he was a high priest and a helper of Zerubbabel. Of the Jews among the people over 24,193 returned. The priests that returned from Babylon numbered over 4,289. The returning Levites numbered over 341. The Nethinim's or temple servants were counted as over 392. The registered ones that had no pedigree or could not show their father's house, and their seed, numbered 652. The register taken that counted priests without pedigree were either left out of the priesthood until it was determined by a priest with the Urin and Thummin. The sub-total of the whole congregation that had returned from Babylon was 42,360 (Ezra 2:64, Nehemiah 7:66). Added to this were the servants and their maids 7,337; and singers, 200. This gave a grand total of 49,897, nearly 50,000 who made up the first expedition out of Babylon.

The Jews' horses, mules, camels, and their asses added up to 8, 136.

The second phase of the return from Babylon happened under Ezra, the priest and scribe. This was after the nearly 50,000 returned, the setting up of the altar in the finished Temple, the restoration of Temple worship, Ezra returned to Judah. Ezra had not been in Jerusalem during the previous events but has returned just after the rebuilding of the Temple was complete.

Ezra returns during the reign of Artazerxes, the same King who gave Nehemiah permission to return to Jerusalem to rebuild the city, which marks the beginning of the great prophecy of the "Seventy weeks of Daniel.[48] After about 5 months they finally reached Jerusalem. There were 1,754 males in Ezra's company in this second expedition. Including unnamed women, Nethinims and Levites, there were well over 2,000 in this second wave.

These are all the returns mentioned in God's Words. There probably were many who did return after this. This was a combination of all 12 tribes and the Levites also. It was not just a return of the two tribes of Judah.

This was the first completed dispersion of Jews from Israel done in the two agonizing stages.

First the northern 10 tribes of Israel were taken to Assyria. After a space of roughly 135 years, the southern two tribes of Judah along with the inhabitants of Jerusalem, or what was left, were carried off to Babylon.

They were returned now only to be thrust out again in about 500 years in the year 70 A.D.

---

[31] Lucenbill, "Ancient Records of Assyria and Babylon." 1926.

[32] Ibid.

[33] Robinson. "History of Israel." 1951. pp 379-380.

[34] Wikipedia. "Assyrian Captivity." en.Wikipedia.org/wiki/Assyrian captivity.

[35] Clarke. Commentary Vol 2. pp 535-6

[36] Ibid. p 536.

[37] Dimont. "Jews, God and History." p 20

[38] From Dake Reference Bible Notes, pp 368-370

[39] Dake. KJV. Notes: pp 370-400

[40] Apposion – an explanatory equivalent.

[41] What is British Israelism?" gotquestions.org. p 2

[42] Robinson, "History of Israel." p 402.

[43] Dake Reference Bible. KJ Version. p 488. Note f, cd 1.

[44] Smith. "Book of Isaiah." Vol. 2 p 175.

[45] Ibid. p 176

[46] Ibid. p 176

[47] McClain. "Daniel's Prophecy of 70 weeks." P 23.

[48] McGee. "Ezra, Nehemiah & Esther." P 46.

CHAPTER 2

THE SEPARATORS

There has been an issue in Christendom that has had an annoying effect, a confusing and irritating effect on me for years. It is finally time to let it out, air dry it, and be able to move on in Christ.

The problem is one of separation. The threat of not separating from error is one that the Israelites faced throughout their history and from which the church is not immune. For the Christian believers to be in ignorance of what the Bible has to teach concerning this vast subject of separation is to insure the victory of the coming apostasy and to vitiate (invalidate) God's plan and will for His born again, blood-bought children.[49]

The doctrine of separation is narrowed appreciably, making the primary point of the investigation, not theological or practical, so much as Biblical.[50]

Dr. Waite then breaks down the doctrine of separation into two parts, as defined both positively and negatively.

A. In a positive fashion, it is to be the believer's complete yieldedness unto his God and Father to do as He alone directs in every avenue of his life.[51]

B. Negative Separation. Negatively considered is the attitude of the believer toward sin and things connected with it that would make him withdraw from anything that is so degraded and made low that it is unbefitting to his walk before God to indulge himself in it.[52]

> *"And the children of Israel, which were come again out of captivity, and all such as had separated themselves unto them from the filthiness of the heathen of the land, to seek the Lord God of Israel,"* (Ezra 6:21)

The separation occurred after the children of Israel returned from Babylon and were grateful to God and were celebrating the Passover once again. But in Ezra 9:1, the non-separation and the discouragement leading to sinful practices was confronted by Ezra. They had intermarried with all the different heathen peoples around them. They plunged back into immorality and idolatry. The returned remnant were very displeasing in God's eyes. This was seventy-five years after the first expedition reached Jerusalem. Ezra was overwhelmed that the first wave of Jews had sunk so low.

There is another low to which the Church has sunk to in these latter days. That is, the failure to separate truth from heresy when it comes to the remnant.

To say that God's remnant pertains to Christians or to God's Church is rank heresy and false doctrine. Why would God's people want to perpetuate some myth without clarifying it for God's people? As stated in the introduction to this study, there is no remnant present today, either in Israel, or either Christian. To state that is in violation of God's doctrine of the remnant. The remnant in the past has been almost all Jewish in totality. It will be the same for the yet as called

Jewish remnant that will come out of the Tribulation.

We are not to concern ourselves with the work that God will do with Israel when the time comes. They will obey keeping His commandments and have the testimony of Jesus Christ.

Besides the accepted meaning of to obey, this (Rev. 12:17) and many other passages containing the command of keeping God's words, echo the truth of the Great Commission that requires all believers to receive, preserve, and obey God's oral and written revelation.[53]

Why should we not be spreading distortions and outright untruths about God's yet to be called eschatological Jewish remnant? Two good reasons are given in Dr. Waite's book.

The reasons for Separation unto God's ways.[54]

a. To keep from falling into sin.

b. To bring their state up to their standing.

No matter how much has been or will be written on the subject examples are all around of so many distinguished evangelicals and Christians, who have a deep knowledge of the Bible, have such a blind, superficial understanding of how great and how often Scripture is violated in this matter. We need to encourage those who can see the truth hidden in plain sight, that God will call a Jewish remnant to be led out and saved out of the Tribulation. Anything less believed is not in God's Bible and therefore heresy.

One needs only to go to the Abrahamic covenant that God made to His people which underlies the whole prophetic question. The promises of God to Abraham of a land, a seed, and a blessing would be everlasting. This covenant, then, necessitates a remnant to be that promised seed, who can occupy the land given that seed and through whom the promised blessing can come.[55] The church has not superceded to fulfill the Abrahamic Covenant. To believe that or to believe the tenets leading up to that conclusion, is worse than the heresy itself. Yet, here, in front of us is proof examined of such danger.

Today, the doctrine of the remnant has been and is under attack by those holding to the amillennial belief. Oswald T. Allis, in "Prophecy and the Church" is one such Amillennialist. Amillennialism teaches that the 1,000 year reign of Christ as found in Revelation 20, is not literal, and the events listed are to be interpreted allegorically or using a spiritualizing method of interpreting prophecy. This method destroys the absolute sense that God intended for his words to be understood. If words do not mean what they say, there is therefore no way to use discernment in determining what they mean. We then do not have a more sure word of prophecy as it says in 2 Peter 1:19, but end up with an unsure word and chaos all around.

The danger, of course, then is affirming that the Church is fulfilling the covenants that God gave to Israel only, and that there will be no further fulfillment thereof. The post-tribulation rapturist cannot uphold the doctrine of the remnant, since their belief is that the Church is going through the Tribulation and becomes the remnant.

The existence of a Jewish Tribulation remnant is inseparable with the covenants God has made with Israel.

Since these covenants were unconditional, their very nature demands the existence of a remnant to whom and through whom these covenants can be fulfilled.[56]

The Palestinian covenant was established by God; "and the Lord thy God will bring thee into the land which thy fathers possessed, and thou shalt possess it;" (Deuteronomy 30:5) This is the basis by which Israel will occupy the land. Again, for this covenant to be fulfilled calls for the existence of a remnant in order to receive it.

God made the Davidic covenant with Israel. This promised an everlasting kingly throne and a kingdom, with a king of the seed of Abraham, (II Samuel 1: 12-16)

> *"Then may also my covenant be broken with David my servant, that he should not have a son to reign upon his throne;"* (Jeremiah 33:21)

It was explained in verse 20 how impossible it was for this covenant to be broken. If it were possible for man to do that then the fact that day and night exists would have to be ended by mankind. It is just not in the power of man to do so. The Davidic covenant, likewise, as the others, demands a remnant, a Jewish remnant, for whom these promises of God can be fulfilled.

The fourth unconditional covenant made by God was the new covenant with Israel. God says of this covenant:

> *"After those days, saith the Lord, I will put my law in their inward parts, and write it in their hearts;...and they shall teach no more every man his neighbor,...saying know the Lord, for they shall all know me,"* (Jeremiah 31: 33, 34)

144

For all the promises to the nation Israel to be fulfilled in the new covenant, there must be a remnant of the nation Israel with whom God may fulfill his word.

The fifth section to this recital of the covenants of God is about the character of God. For God to make unconditional covenants with Israel that takes no effort or work from the Israelites, they must rely solely on the performance of God for them to have any effect. God's reputation and very character is at stake. If God cannot bring about what He has promised, He would be proven to be a liar. The integrity of God, then, makes the existence of a remnant necessary.[57]

How important it is to understand God's plan and that plan called for two remnants. The first would be the one that has been in the beginning of this dispensation (covered later) and the Jewish Eschatological remnant which will be yet to be called in the next. Between these two remnants are where the world is and where the Church is.

The Body of the Lord Jesus Christ is composed of the believing Jews and Gentiles and that through the preaching of the Gospel of Grace, not only are sinners of the Gentiles added to that Body, but also Jews who believe on the Lord Jesus Christ.[58]

As soon as a Jew believes he ceases to be a Jew. His hope is no longer national and earthly, but heavenly; he belongs no longer to the earthly Jerusalem, but to the heavenly; he has, like the believing Gentile, nothing to do with the law, its ordinances and ceremonies. It is impossible to speak of a remnant of Israel at this time.[59] Paul, in

Romans 11:5 wrote about the remnant in the present, "...there is a remnant," at the beginning of the Dispensation of Grace. This will be discussed later.

> *"And they are informed of thee, that thou teachest all the Jews which are among the Gentiles to forsake Moses, saying that they ought not to circumcise their children, neither to walk after their customs."* (Acts 21:21)

This is a good preaching by Paul. Where is that today? Is it in the mainstream church, fundamentalist church, or the Messianic Jewish churches? These things are not true in the Messianic churches, for example. They are not uniform on many, if not all of their beliefs. They must get back to the Bible and what Paul actually said about Jesus Christ and that Christ Jesus is the only way to salvation (Acts 4:12)

The believing Jew at this time (2020s) is not "gentilized," as has been pressed so much from certain sides, but he becomes a member of the Body of the Lord Jesus Christ, and shares with every other believer a heavenly hope, a heavenly destiny.

However, there seems to be a problem today with some in the Body of Christ. There is no separation between the acknowledgement of the remnant and the Christian, born-again members of the church. There is no present remnant, right, so who and why is that term substituted and used for born-again believers?

There have been questions raised between myself and Pastor Waite, my own Pastor, on this very subject. I wrote an e-mail on May 9, 2019, some of which it stated:

> "From the time of Christ's rejection by Israel until the time when God deals specifically with Israel again in the seventieth week, it is not possible to refer to a remnant of the nation Israel. In the Body of Christ all national distinctions disappear. All Jews who are saved are not saved into a national relationship, but into a relationship in Christ in that body of believers. Therefore, there is no continuing remnant of,

The e-mail continues:

> "There are those who say the church is the remnant today, according to Romans 11:5. The contrasts between the church and Israel, the concept of the church as a mystery, a distinctive relationship of the church to Christ, and the specified purpose of the church all make such an interpretation impossible.

> "The blindness of Israel is a temporary blindness, and because of it God cannot have a remnant with whom the covenants will be fulfilled. To say the church would be fulfilling the promises and covenants of God would be supersessionism, a very serious heresy."

Another e-mail to Dr. Waite sent on August 18, 2018

> "Pastor, I just don't understand (ed. I do, much more now) why Dr. Spence keeps referring to the remnant as the church in these final days. There is nothing in the Bible that supports this. It is unfounded, unbiblical and very confusing.

> "I am confused every time I hear it. He (Dr. Spence) used the term at least 14 times at DBS (Dean Burgon Society) without any explanation. You mean to tell me that everyone present and

listening had perfect understanding of each use of the term? Not possible. Everything I read on the end-time remnant, people actually shy away of the term as being applied to the church. The closeness of our personal relationship with Christ and Christ with us precludes Him thinking of us as mere leftovers, or what is left. If anyone thinks that the remnant is the church and that the church will be counted as the remnant going through the Tribulation, and that the church is Israel, that person is a replacement theologist.

In Him, Charles Kriessman "

The reply I got from Dr. Waite is interesting and from somewhere right out of a redefined King James Bible.

On August 31, 2018, Dr. D. A. Waite wrote:

"Dear Charles:

"You are, of course, entitled to your opinion on this matter, Charles, and I am sure you will still differ with me and others on it, as you have in the past, no matter what we might say or write about it. There is, below, an accurate definition of the English word "remnant." It is accurate to use the English word, "remnant: to refer to those very few ministers and other today who stand for the former sound doctrinal and practical principles of former Fundamentalist Christians. This English term can never be restricted only to is use in the Bible for faithful Israelites and never used in the English Bible language for anything or anyone else. I believe Dr. Spence is correct, and I agree with on it, with his special use of this English word "remnant," when he talks and writes about it."

"In Christ, Pastor D.A. Waite"

Rem-nant/remnant

Noun 1. A small remaining quantity of something.

I had to reply:

September 1, 2018

Pastor, you used the word "English" 5 times in your email.

Is there a separation of the "English" word usage or remnant from the Greek/Hebrew usage of the word for remnant?

Waiting on the reply, the scriptures yielded a helpful resolution.

"'these were more noble than those in Thessalonica, in that they received the word with all readiness of mind, and searched the scriptures daily, whether those things were true." (Acts 17:11)

Pastor's reply: September 1, 2018

Yes, I believe it is, Charles. In Christ.

Incredible. According to the Oxford dictionary, online, the definition for remnant, under "Christian theology" is a small minority of people who will remain faithful to God and so be saved (in allusion to biblical prophecies concerning Israel). Now, why couldn't he say that? Instead, the Pastor, my pastor, sides with a separator, a supersessionist and a non-dispensationalist. Let's look closer at Dr. Spence and what he has to say, shall we?

Dr. Spence

Turning now to Dr. H. T. Spence. Exodus 26:12 is the first instance that the word remnant is used in the Bible.

"And the remnant that remaineth of the curtain of the tent..." (Exodus 26:12)

Moses had been called by God and he went into the cloud up Mount Sinai and was there with the Lord forty days and forty nights (Exodus 24:18). God gave to Moses, thus Israel, the blueprint for the Tabernacle and the garments for the priests out of the offerings that the children of Israel were to give for the tabernacle, included materials for the curtains or coverings of the Tabernacle. The four separate coverings consisted of ten curtains of fine linen; colored blue, purple, and scarlet. There were to be eleven curtains of goat's hair. The third curtain was made up of ram's skins dyed red. The fourth and final curtain was to be outer covering of badger skin.[60] Let it be noted that badgers were found in the Holy Land area, according to Unger. However, their skins are and were not suited to be the outer covering of the Tabernacle. The Hebrew word, *tahash,* can come from the Arabic cognate, *tuhas,* which describes the Dugong.[61] The Dugong was a marine-like animal which had whale-like qualities. It was quite plentiful on the coral (colored) banks of the Red Sea.

The Dugongs usually averaged 8 to 10 feet long and were between 500 and 900 pounds each. They had thick, smooth skin which was brownish to dark gray as they aged. These skins would have served well as an outer layer for the roof of the

150

Tabernacle. Though there is no direct proof that the skins of the dugong were used for the Tabernacle, the challenge is set out for any proof to the opposite, or else we will have to wait on the confirmation from our Lord.

From the Scripture it states that there would be leftover parts of the linen and goat's hair curtains. These would overlap and hang over the backside of the tented tabernacle. The coverings of the ram skins dyed red and the Dugong skins would complete the four layers of the Tabernacle's coverings.

Since this is the first use of the word remnant in the Bible, its use is very significant. The Tabernacle in the wilderness pointed into the future when God would dwell with His people on the earth.

> *I will dwell in the midst of the children of Israel for ever, and my holy name, shall the house of Israel no more defile..."* (Ezekiel 43:7)

Ever since the Jews were brought together and recognized as the nation Israel, at the first Passover, the remnant passing through Scripture was and is strictly Jewish, except in rare passages. From the beginning use of the word remnant it pertains to the nation Israel only and to the end of the Bible in Revelation it pertains exclusively to the Jews and Israel with Christ Jesus in the midst of the children of Israel.

Dr. H. T. Spence, President of Foundations Bible College, in Dunn, North Carolina, embarks on a brief review of the history of the remnant. This is found in "Straightway" Magazine of January-March 2012. He begins with the time of Hezekiah and the

Kingdom of Judea, when Israel was backed up into Jerusalem.

It's true when he mirrors Isaiah when he saw the remnant as being very small. But it is applied to a group within Jerusalem, and referred to a small group that survived the Assyrian attacks under Tiglath-Pileser III. The remnant mainly applies to the small groups that returned to Israel after captivity, not before. Isaiah writes about the return of the remnant as the remnant that was out of Babylon, as well as an end-time remnant of Jews who would populate the Kingdom.

Spence writes: the post-exilic biblical writings of Ezra, Nehemiah, Haggai, and Zechariah consistently refer to the Jews who have returned from the Babylonian captivity as the remnant. This is very true about all of the main verses of the Bible pertaining to the remnant. He also rightly states the existence of the remnant is said to be due to God himself. He then states; the remnant then are the true people of God. This is in Paul's time and any remnant is Jewish, and it is not the remnant, they are part of the church. Paul called it a remnant in Roman's 11:5, according to the election of grace. That group of Jews and believers were in the Asian church and would be dispersed in the 70 A.D. Diaspora.

Dr. Spence speculates about the return from Babylon, and about the importance of the remnant (this is what he says Daniel said) that were to be found in various times of prophecy. It is non-dispensational zig-zagging through history with the remnant that is confusing. Then all of a sudden it is seventy years later and a godly remnant (about

50,000) Jews returned to Jerusalem to rebuild first the temple, and later the walls. The order of restoring Jerusalem is correct but it is disjointed from the narrative and hard to follow. It is not Biblical to call it a godly remnant that returned from Babylon. There were priests and Levites present but by the time Ezra arrived they had intermarried with heathens and fallen into idol worship once again and needed to get right according to the law.

There is a New Testament continuation to Spence's biblical history of the remnant. He states: "in the New Testament, it is evident that the gospel is only accepted by a remnant of people."[62] There's that word again, handled very loosely. The gospel is accepted by thousands, and they became born-again Christians, and belonged to the church. They are not the remnant, or a remnant, they are saints of the Lord, not leftovers. He further states: "the wholesale falling away in the public church is in contrast to the continuing biblical remnant."[63]

What does that mean? Could a pastor put that statement in his next sermon and feed it to his flock? Would they understand? He then brings in Matthew 24, the Olivet Discourse, to believers about things that are signs now but it is directed to the Jews who will be alive then before 70 A.D. and in the Tribulation. It has very little if anything besides being aware, to the church, and everything to do with future events, after the church has been removed. For example, Matthew 24 Verse 13 has to do with Jewish souls who hear the preaching of the 144,000 and endure until Christ calls them out of Israel to flee to the mountains to be kept by Christ for the duration of the Tribulation. He further states: "As the Old Testament declared that only a remnant of the Jewish nation would come through, so the New Testament indicates that only a remnant of the visible church would come through; all else would be lost." This is muddled theology. Come through what? The cheesecake eating marathon? This is ludicrous, there are no Scriptures given for whatever this is. There is no end-time remnant in Revelation 3:2,4, as he states.

For all the misuse of the word remnant as pertaining to the New Testament that Dr. Spence writes about, it is very curious and suspect since there is no remnant today. Israel became a state and has been re-gathering all Jews that will come back to Israel. We cannot be part of a remnant that doesn't exist. That is not possible.

According to Spence, the Old Testament Jews turned into the New Testament church. That is, the church is now the remnant, which was entirely a Jewish entity. The church is not Israel, has not become Israel, and illustrates one of the grave dangers of Dr. Spence's theology. The word supersessionism comes from the English verb "to supersede" from the Latin verb "sedere," to sit, plus "super" upon. It thus signifies one thing, being replaced or supplanted by another.[64]

Strangely, there is no mention of any covenants or covenants being fulfilled by Christ for the Jews. One of the premises of Replacement theology is:

> The promises, blessings, and covenants once given to the Jews have been taken away and given to the church. The Jews are still subject

to the curses found in the Bible, as a result of their rejection of Christ.[65]

What else are we to suppose, since Dr. Spence's writings are saturated with the church as remnant, and the remnant church, titles?

The Jews are a separate people to whom pertains the adoption, the glory, the covenants, the promises, the law, and the service of God (Roman's 9:4). God has not revoked the gifts and calling to His people (Romans 11:29). There are numerous places in the New Testament that only refer to Israel and not the church. Paul is talking to believers in Romans 10:1 and prays that Israel might be saved, for it does not pertain to the church to be saved who already were saved. The promises made to Abraham in Genesis 12: 1-3 are everlasting promises made to Israel. There are promises God has made to Israel and the Jewish people and God's affirmation of these is found in Jeremiah 31:35-37.

> *"In these days they shall say no more, the fathers have eaten a sour grape, and the children's teeth are set on edge."* (Jeremiah 31:29)

God's promises to a future Israel will be fulfilled according to Romans 11: 25-27.

> *"The error of Replacement Theology is like a cancer in the church that not only caused it to violate God's word concerning the Jewish people and Israel, but it made us into instruments of hate, not love, in God's name. Yet, it is not too late to change our ways and rightly relate to the Jewish people and Israel today."*[66]

Dr. Spence would do well to not use the word remnant in his writings concerning the church and born-again Christians. For one thing, it is tedious to scrutinize and undo the knots of semantics that have been used by any semanticist. The meaning of the words used should be thought out and rendered understandable in all aspects to the intended receivers of those words. No amount of abuse, theologically, economically, or otherwise will result in the total suppression or annihilation of the Jews. The Nazi's tried that and failed. God has already planned for Israel's future, supersessionalists need not worry.

1. All Israel will be saved. (Romans 11:26)
2. Israel will look on the Messiah and accept him. (Zechariah 12:10)
3. Israel will be forgiven of all sin. (Romans 11:27)

Do not make the mistake that the future prophesies meant for Israel will be fulfilled in the church.

> *"I say then, hath God cast away his people?"* (Romans 11:1)

Today's church is a terrible disgrace that started long ago in the early church with Justin Martyr. This false doctrine of supersessionism, the replacement of Israel with the church is diabolical and has gripped the entirety of the mainstream church to the point that more than a majority of church-goers support their claims. Whether supersessionists have made their case or not, the damage inflicted upon low-information Christians is evidence of this present evil. Christians need to be taught, and also learn on their own the Biblical revelation that God has given us concerning latter times Israel and its restoration.

One final point before leaving off with Dr. Spence. On October 3-7. 2018, Dr. H.T. Spence hosted a conference at Foundations Bible College and Seminary entitled: "A Congress for the Christian Remnant." After what the reader has read in this Chapter 2, the title and its implications should be self-explanatory, but if not, the reader knows what to do.

A phone call was placed to Dr. Spence after reading about the so-called remnant church, etc., on or about the middle of 2012. Questions were asked then about their conference on the Christian remnant and if there were any Scriptures to read and learn about this Christian remnant. The answer, of course, was that there were none, but that further searching may yield some answers. It was asked if it should be more accurately named, "A Congress for the Christian Church?" Crickets.

Anyway, in attendance for the conference in 2018, were Dr. Waite and Dr. Kirk DiVietro. Now before delving in any further, Dr. DiVietro is a very fine pastor. He was one of the pastors that accompanied Pastor John F. Kelly of South Kingston, RI, who was killed in an ambush near Baghdad, Iraq, on February 24, 2004. There were four Baptist preachers there in Iraq, assisting in the starting of a Baptist church in Iraq.

Dr. DiVietro is a very brave pastor, willing to put up his life to help set up a church so that people could hear the message of the Gospel. Dr. DiVietro is quoted, "Division is caused by those who leave a once held position."

"His mantra is "Scholarship is the art of making complicated things simple rather than making simple things complicated. It can be a wonderful servant, but a terrible master."[67]

Dr. DiVietro was sharing his knowledge at the same Congress for the Christian Remnant in Dunn, North Carolina. The brochure for the event states: only a remnant of God's people are to be found who are living for Christ...thus for the hope of encouraging the Remnant...

So, I asked Dr. DiVietro about the present day remnant and if it was fulfilling the covenants and promises of God? I said in my email of September 24, 2018, to him:

"In 2006, or before, he (Dr. Spence) started writing about a Christian "Remnant."

"Instantly I was in a confused state about this subject. Everything else he wrote was impeccable, but this bothered me for months. I think it was 2011 or 2012 I called Dr. Spence for an explanation. I wish I had a recording of that conversation because it left me more confused and with more questions. I remember that I asked for the Scriptures to which he based this premise upon. That was sloughed off as not being important.

"I have questioned Pastor D.A. Waite on this point but he has closed his mind to it. Dr. Waite also bases this concept of the Christian Remnant on no Scriptures whatsoever. This amazes me because everything Pastor Waite teaches and preaches on is based entirely on the words of God. He just says that he agrees with Spence in this matter. What I gather is that he separates the use of the "ENGLISH" word remnant from any biblical text underlying the word remnant. He has confirmed to me that this is so.

"I believe that there was a historical remnant in the past, that there is NO remnant, Jewish or Christian, in the present, and that there will be a called remnant by God in the future. I would like to get your thoughts on this subject to shed any light on my confusion. I thought that the church were the called out ones of saved Gentiles and saved Jews that God is preparing as his spotless bride. Please correct me if I am wrong.

In Christ, Dr. Charles J. Kriessman III"

Dr. DiVietro's response:

"On its face I do not understand your objections to the use of the word remnant. I have no problem extending that concept to believers today in a day of apostasy as an informal identification. I do not know if this is Dr Spence's basis for using the term or not, but I am not offended by the term. DiVietro

I came to these three pastors in a humble spirit seeking answers and transparency. What I got was condescension or patronizing as to someone beneath their rank or dignity. I just don't understand and why Dr. Spence keeps referring to the Remnant as the church in these final days. There is nothing in the Bible that supports this. It is unfounded, unbiblical, and was very confusing. There are no doubts that if someone thinks that the Remnant is the church, and calls it the Remnant Church, and that the church is Israel, that person is a Replacement theologist.

This chapter is called strangely, the Separators, since some Christians, great men of God, wish to separate the word remnant from its

God intended meaning and redefine it to apply to a totally new concept. It is as if we are to believe in this certain way or definition of remnant but hang on to and acknowledge every other historical and eschatological definition of the word. It is a type of henotheism in Christian circles. If we, as born-again Christians are to be remnant, then just come out and teach that as clear, Biblical doctrine. Do not force people to be renitent just so a false belief can be proven right. How the Bible is interpreted determines one's theology.

One last note before moving on. Dr. Jack Moorman wrote an excellent forty-five page booklet entitled, "The Beginning, Baptism, Body, and Bride; a Local Church Error Refuted." Acts 11:15; Galatians 3:27; Ephesians 5:30; and Revelation 22:17 depict God's view of the church in four key words: beginning, baptized, body, and bride. He lists nine (9) Post-Pentecost names given to the church: 1) The church, 2) the body, 3) a building,4) a house, 5) a temple, 6) an assembly, 7) a gathering, 8) a priesthood, 9) a bride, virgin, wife.

Not once in that listing is the name remnant used. That is because of the very simple fact that the remnant or a remnant or any such semantical rendering of the word is not a name for the church. The only times you will hear Dr. Waite use the term remnant is when Romans 9:27 and 11:25 are being taught on. If one attends Dr. Spence's church, the word remnant is bantered about frequently with the full understanding that the remnant is the church. This author deeply believes that the nine terms listed, especially the names Body and Bride, should be used exclusively for the church so as to avoid any confusion or misguidance.

> *"For we are members of his body, of his flesh, and of his bones. This is a great mystery: but I speak concerning Christ and the Church."* (Ephesians 5: 30, 32)

In a tangible and visible sense the local church is the body, building, house, temple, assembly, gathering, priesthood, and perhaps bride of Christ.[68]

> *"And he is the head of the body, the church:"* (Colossians 1:18a)

Using the term remnant for church demeans the work of Christ in which the Lord is sanctifying His born-again believers. It spits in the eye of God who gave His son for the lost souls so that their sins may be forgiven. He is cleaning the church which is the body of believers, and He loves every one of them.

> *"That he might present it to himself a glorious church, not having spot or wrinkle, or any such thing; but that it should be holy and without blemish.:"* (Ephesians 5:27)

We rejoice in being the church, the Body of Christ, having such a blessed God who died for it, and is its glorious head. He has saved us, reconciled us to the Father, and planted us and built us up and established us in the faith.

> *"Who now rejoice in my sufferings for you, and fill up that which is behind of the afflictions of Christ in my flesh for his body's sake, which is the church:"* (Colossians 1:24)

Decline of Dispensational Teaching

A paper written by Pastor Tod Brainard centers on "Progressive Dispensationalism" a book written by Blaising and Bock. They perceived that there is a wide gulf between dispensationalist theology, and covenant theology that should not exist. What they first decided on was a dilution of the doctrine of the church and the doctrine of Israel. That is done by watering down the accepted distinctions between Israel and the church. They endowed the Christ bought church with earthly kingdom characteristics. They deny this present time as being of the Church Age and give an Old Testament spin to the church.

The mysteries center on Christ Jesus and the Church.

> "...the preaching of Jesus Christ, according to the revelation of the mystery, which was kept secret since the world began." (Romans 16:25)

> "But we speak the wisdom of God in a mystery, even the hidden wisdom, which God ordained before the world unto our glory;" (Corinthians 2:7)

> "Having made known unto us the mystery of his will,..." (Ephesians 2:9)

Progressive Dispensationalism is drawing in many neo-evangelical and some Fundamentalist teachers and professors at seminaries and Bible colleges. This is allowing them to move away from the anchors of the faith and preventing them from rightly dividing the word of God. The clear teaching of the revelation of God given in dispensationalism is muddied and nearly absent in Progressive Dispensationalism.

Clarity in Interpretation

How the Bible is interpreted determines one's system of theology.[69] The Bible is the divine revelation of God through the Holy Spirit, through human authors, according to the purpose of God.

> "... a workman not to be ashamed, rightly dividing the Word of Truth." (2 Timothy 2:15)

Studying the words of God in a consistent, literal, grammatical-historical method leads naturally to a dispensational framework of Scripture.[70] Which type of interpretation is employed will determine the views of doctrines and relationship in the Bible.

Church growth methodologies employed by modern churches today erode the truths of classic dispensationalism, and as a result most conservative mainline churches are employing covenant theology and Progressive Dispensationalism. This leads to earthly methods in dealing with people and their problems. They think of the church in earthly, modernistic terms and fail to treat God's institution as heavenly. The classic dispensationalist proclaims heavenly truths that look beyond the earthly and material, to the eternal.[71]

> "While we look not at the things which are seen, but at the things which are not seen: for the things which are seen are temporal; but the things which are not seen are eternal." (2 Corinthians 4:18)

The teaching of eternal things would include: ministry of reconciliation, servant training, equipping saints for heaven, knowledge of the Holy Spirit, prophetic preaching, etc.

Rejection of Present Apostasy

Just to review: rightly dividing the truth is from the Greek, *orthotomeo*, meaning to set straight, handle rightly. It is used only in 2 Timothy 2:15, directing the student of Scripture to give words and passages in the Bible the true meaning, when preaching or writing about them. It entails not only giving the true meaning but as importantly providing the true application of those truths to the various times and classes of people These, then, must be divided dispensationally, prophetically, and historically with regard to classes and subjects. Interpret the Bible literally where possible, if not possible it is figurative, and getting at the literal truth by the figurative language is in order.

Some of the results of not rightly dividing show up in the progressive movement and within their churches. This type of Progressive Dispensationalist/Covenant people are stubborn to accept the fact of the present worldwide apostasy of the church. They instead push for an end time revival based upon allegorized Old Testament Scriptures which relates to Israel and the Millennium.

Today there is a lack of preaching on the great prophetic themes in the Bible. There was a steep decline in prophetic teaching through the twentieth century until the present where such is very scarce and disjointed at best. Teaching on the

Pre-Tribulational Rapture is rare and it was that blessed hope that spurred Christians on to pure living before the coming of the Lord. Now the Christian landscape is strewn with the feel-good, don't judge sin seminars. We are encouraged, all the saints:

> *"...stand fast, and hold the traditions which ye have been taught, whether by word, or our epistle."* (2 Thessalonians 2:15)

Instead of solid biblical, doctrinal, prophetic teaching, there are substituted methodologies, practical growth methods, psychological solution and programs, meditation, techniques, and seminars. It is truly a Laodicean Church situation (Revelation 3:14-22.) Today's condition of the church is compromised to the point of being ecumenical, global church apostasy. Without dispensational preaching together with heretical teachers and preachers, there is only ignorance and confusion. Unless the church snaps to and involves itself in Holy Ghost led glorifying of Christ Jesus all precious truth will be abandoned.

Separation from error is a primary Christian duty; to avoid all false and ungodly teaching is to protect oneself spiritually. A Christian cannot maintain God's truth without taking action on separation from the Devil's lies and having discipline in his/her walk with God.

The term "remnant" is used six times in the New Testament, and translated "remnant" by the Greek Words, *kataleimma, leimma*, (the root), and *loipos*. According to James W. Watts, [72] many scholars have heightened the remnant's role in the New Testament and claimed that remnant theology is central to Christian's appropriating the traditions and theology of Israel for the church. Watts seemingly has uncovered evidence for the church replacing Israel or Replacement Theology. As a result of this, it is believed that the followers of Jesus identified with the remnant in order to trace their continuity back generations, to those in the Old Testament.[73]

So, these Christians want to trace their heritage back to Abraham, Moses, and the prophets and then they can consider themselves to be, the True Israel. This gives them such a wide scope of tradition makes the 'sweeping theories" of remnant applications, especially carried on in the New Testament.

R.E. Clements, one of the proponents to the "sweeping remnant theories" wrote: "The importance of the concept of a remnant to Pauline thought...to interpret the Old Testament Scriptures to provide the foundations of a Christian theology.[74] Others who have thought the remnant theme of central importance to the NT message were Frank, Skagg, Paul K. Jewell, and John Bright.

T. W. Manson outdistanced these by saying that a saving remnant was the key to the New Testament. In his full-blown remnant theology he traced the theme of remnant from Isaiah through the "I" worshiper in Psalms, the son of man in Daniel, down to the son of man in the gospels. He wrongly surmised that the remnant is the form of the kingdom in this world.[75]   He also tied the word "Man" with "son of man" in order to lump everything into one concept of the remnant.

Watts explains there are three things underlying the "sweeping theories, remnant theme's" importance which is exaggerated in the New Testament. First, that remnant theology is central in the Old Testament, that claims of a remnant were vital in ancient Judaism, and finally the New Testament identified the church with Israel. There's that supersessionism raising its head again. There are extensive reviews of the origin's theory, being traced by Staff, Jewell, and Bright.

Widespread belief by NewTestament scholars that there is deep importance about the "sweeping theme" in first century Judaism, gets much exposure. Ben F. Meyer states: "Remnant theology shaped the self-understanding of all Judaic sectarian communities contemporary with the early church. The first Christians were no exceptions. [76]

T. W. Manson, argued that the Pharisees especially claimed to be the faithful remnant of Israel.[77]

By having in contrast the notion that in first century Palestine the idea that the church is the remnant bolsters the New Testament church claim to the same.

Was there a pervading Old Testament stream of thought by the individual, and radical sects, who thought of themselves as the exclusive eschatological remnant? Some refused to accept that premise to build their theology on.

Here is where we must distinguish the differences between a "historical remnant" and the "eschatological remnant." A "historical" remnant is any one of many groups which survive a catastrophe, usually one considered to have resulted from God's judgment on His people. The "eschatological" remnant is composed of those who remain after the final judgment on the wicked.[78]

The distinction was derived from Hasel, who once attached earlier tendencies to distinguish "secular" and "religious" remnants in the OT. He studied the remnant in Amos and Isaiah and found it necessary to separate historical from eschatological uses. He summarized what he found: "the early history of the remnant motif or theme in the Hebrew Bible shows that it was originally not eschatological and that it did not arise in the cult... In Amos it received for the first time a distinctly eschatological usage. The eschatological or holy remnant, purified by divine purging, was for Isaiah an object of faith and future reality."[79]

The Old Testament identifies many historical remnants. However, all these sweeping remnant theorists recognize that there was no established eschatological remnant. They concluded that was true for two reasons. The first was the attempt in avoiding a self-righteous stance. The second was the Jewish belief in the restoration of Israel. Mainly it is for the simple explanation that the end-time future remnant has not been called yet.

In light of the way the separate remnants of Israel are identified and handled historically, it was claimed that New Testament remnant usage had prejudiced modern readers. The bottom line is that the remnant interpretation in the New Testament is simply misinterpretation. By positioning the theology in the remnant of the Jewish context of the remnant, it may or may not be based on the Jewish context. The only true and firm conviction that ever comes of that is that the New Testament identifies the church as the true Israel. Jewett, for instance, gave room to the conflicting views on the subject but surmised, "In the end the New Testament is enough: the early Christians, for all their Jewish antecedents, believed that the Church, including the Gentiles, was the true people of God, the heir of Israel's election."[80]

There are just endless authors who suggest and write on this very view. Is there any other alternative? When the belief that the New Testament links together the church as Israel, the application of remnant terminology to the church is usually automatically assumed.[81]

About that transition in theology. H.H. Rowley says: "that the church claimed that it was the spiritual Israel and the heir of the election, the remnant that alone could claim the promises reinforced by those of the Gentiles who shared its faith, is hardly to be gainsaid.[82] He added that never is the church's election thought to be as a rival to that as Israel, but as a continuation of that election, to which the church had become heir.[83]

Others, looking through the New Testament, searching for the relation between Israel and the church, have decided that there is no equating the two together.[84] They did find a gradual drift towards that equality by the use of descriptive terms in the Bible for Israel to the church.[85] This involved a suspected highly developed Christology which traced a scheme through to early books of the New Testament that downplayed and diminished Judaism and its future expectations. In its more "inferior" standing it needed rightfully to be replaced by the church which would claim the title 'True Israel.'[86]

The overarching revelation of such investigations reveals the complexity of Israel and the church and their separate functions and responsibilities to God, makes it too simplistic to say that the church is the heir to Israel. Through the impossibility of that, the remnant theme is seen to have been caught up in the transition of transposed titles. The sweeping remnant theorists must once again scramble to come up with data that explicitly names the church as the eschatological remnant of Israel.

These, and there are more, challenges to the sweeping remnant theories platform are only the result of the lack of evidence for such in the New Testament. One cannot use arguments from the historical theological remnant studies to shore up the stance of the remnant being the domain of the church over Israel. There has been much more emphasis on the restoration hope for Israel, and less on the Jewish remnant when examined. The search for the true claims of the eschatological Jewish remnant show a lack of attempts to completely define it accurately. This may only show that the theme of the remnant has been misused and is not all that prevalent in Christendom anyway.

Some in Christendom have seen sweeping theories of the remnant in passages in Matthew through John in the New Testament. Since any reference does not exist in the gospels of any remnant terminology, the ideas of Jesus Christ and

John the Baptist have to be constructed to make it appear as if they do.

There is the opinion, which is pretty widespread, that John the Baptist had as his baptizing ministry the purpose of fathering the eschatological remnant out of Israel. Such was the religious climate in the first century that John's ministry had this as an obvious outcome. Ben Meyer postulated: "through baptism in token of conversion, he sought to create the remnant of true Israel.[87] Meyer qualified his statement, characterizing John's (the Baptist) preaching as an "open remnant, not exclusive or particularistic but offering a universal invitation.[88] G.F. Hasel also agreed that John the Baptist gathered the remnant but the message was for everyone.

More commentators see John's ministry in terms of remnant theology in its relation to contemporary Judaism. Joachin Jeremias theorized that the Pharisees, the Essenes, and the other first century cults were all busy trying to establish the remnant. Along with Meyer, Gloege reached the same conclusion after studying Old Testament passages on the remnant. Those who do not see John the Baptist immersed in remnant terminology, reason that he attracted people with the method of salvation to a broad sectarian population. Some people see the remnant, and some people do not.

Research can show that claims to being the eschatological remnant were not common back in the first century. Having realized this glaring fact changed the way many perceived that John the Baptist was not calling out an eschatological remnant after all. Upon investigation of John's ministry of preaching and baptizing, there is little or no proof he ever used remnant themes.

From Matthew 3:12 we surmise that the wheat may very well be referring to the remnant but this work belongs to the Lord Jesus Christ, not John. There is coming judgment, and John knows this, and he is not calling out the remnant.

There are those who seek to find any teachings of Christ Jesus in regards to the remnant theme, but find it a tough road to explain the lack of such references. However, people give it that ole' college try. Meyer suggests that from all the teaching of coming judgment, that that is the conclusion one comes to as a witness to the remnant.

Some then think, since Christ Jesus talked in the context of judgment, therefore, and it was to the judgment of Israel he mostly directed his charges, the question of the remnant is a fact. Some have been so bold as to say Jesus had in His mind the remnant context in regard to the calling of the twelve apostles. Christopher Rowland goes so far as to say, "The twelve were the faithful remnant of the twelve tribes.[89] There are others, but what they have said about Jesus and the remnant does not have a large following or influence.

Critics of these people and their view of the remnant in the gospels are directed at two things. First, the many passages that are said to be remnant verses, are attacks on and not in favor of said theories on remnant beliefs. The examples used are the separation parables of the wheat and tares and of the dragnet. But these are last judgment events and carry an implicit warning against exclusive and particularist sectarian practices.[90] These ideas seem to convey that the notion of a "holy remnant" being actively gathered by the Lord from Israel is not feasible.

It is noteworthy that all the ones trying to squeeze out of the Lord everything that is remnant-oriented, could just as well fit into a restoration context as well. It is found that proponents of a remnant theology opposed Jesus' ministry.

Secondly, against remnant theology being taught by Jesus, does suggest that the restoration of Israel is actually the framework that dominated the Lord's mission here on earth.

Was there remnant theology in the Lord's teachings while here on earth? There was definitely restoration teaching, that Israel would go through the Tribulation and refined with the remnant emerging to enter the Kingdom with Christ their King. If it was the model Christ based his ministry upon has dominated theologian thought throughout the Age of Grace. Romans 11:16-29 describes the turning from their blindness of unbelief (Israel), to being forgiven and the nation being saved and existing in the millennium. The theme of the remnant as Israel and the restoration of the nation of Israel walk side-by-side and present no conflict between them.

Many writers have noted the calling of the twelve apostles as the possible start of the formation of the remnant. There is no doubt that the formation of the apostles was the sign to Israel that they could be in the good graces of God once again. Their rejection of that offer has led to their blindness and plagues them to this day. Again, this blindness, due to their rejection of their Messiah who was present among them, will not turn to sight until Israel sees their Messiah as the Lord Jesus Christ, immediately after the Tribulation.

> *"And I will pour upon the house of David, and upon the inhabitants of Jerusalem, the spirit of grace and of supplications: and they shall look upon me whom they have pierced, and they shall mourn for him, as one mourneth for his only son, and shall be in bitterness for him, as one that is in bitterness for his firstborn."* (Zechariah 12:10)

Many Bible interpreters have linked the formation of the twelve apostles as the restoration of the twelve tribes of Israel. In Jesus' time there were twelve tribes, and they were all part of the rejection. The linking of the number twelve with restoration was threaded all the way to an early anti-Christian polemic. Stanton traced this progression through Matthew 23:29, the testament of the twelve and Justin Martyr, and that the punishment of Israel by God is immediately followed by the hope of eventual restoration.[91] This pattern of judgment and then restoration would seem to be the pattern whether a remnant needs to be involved at all still remains the mystery. All of this is still fueling the conflict of remnant theology being a part of Christ's teaching and being a first century concern at all.

It would seem that the restoration of Israel back into the plan of God for Israel would seem to be paramount. Christ said Himself that He was sent to the House of Israel to save that which was lost. All the while, the Creator realized He needed a remnant to be holy and to continue to serve Him to fulfill the covenants made to Israel.

God chose Israel to be His witnesses of Him to the rest of the world which was in darkness. They were to be His shining lights to His beacon of light of salvation to the world. This necessitated that they recognize and believe in their Messiah or die in their sins.

> *"I said therefore unto you, that ye shall die in your sins: for if ye believe not that I am he, ye shall die in your sins.* (John 8:24)

The Lord Jesus Christ is reaching out to Israelites with open arms, begging them to recognize him as Messiah. This aspect of God's love for Israel and the message to each and every Jew, will be the same and will continue until the Nation of Israel looks upon the One with the nail-pierced hands and receives Him as their own.

The argument by writers concerning the remnant will go on. It must be guarded against applying a comprehensive, one size fits all definition for the remnant. What elements wrongly taken from the gospels, especially Matthew, to bolster the sweeping remnant theory needs to be cautiously avoided. These broad paths inevitably lead to the conclusion that the church and Israel are theologically interchangeable and that the church is Israel and, therefore, the Remnant. Misguided definitions, stemming from misguided theology leads to thinking that the remnant theme is found in every gospel or Scripture reference. It cannot all relate to Israel, Christ, the twelve apostles, and the whole of Christendom.

[49] Waite. "Biblical Separation." p 1

[50] Ibid. p 1

[51] Ibid. p 2

[52] Waite. "Biblical Separation." P 2

[53] Brandenburg. Ed. "Thou shalt keep them." p 113

[54] Waite. "Biblical Separation." p 9

[55] Pentecost. "Things to come." p 291

[56] Pentecost. "Things to Come." p 291

[57] Pentecost. "Things to Come." p 292

[58] Gaebelein. "The Remnant." 1912. p 24

[59] Ibid. p 24

[60] Exodus 25: 4, 5

[61] "Dugong." Wikipedia, accessed 7/15/18. 11:37 A.M.

[62] Spence. Straightway Magazine. Jan-Mar 2012. P4.

[63] Ibid. p 15

[64] Wikipedia. "Supersessionism."

[65] Clarence Wagner. "The error of Replacement theology." p 1

[66] Clarence Wagner. "Bridges for Peace. "Speech 2003.

[67] DBS Spotlight

[68] Moorman. "The Church" p 29

[69] Brainard. "Decline of Dispensational Teaching"

[70] Ibid.

[71] Ibid.

[72] Watts, James W. "The Remnant Theme")

[73] Ibid. p 109

[74] Ibid. p 110

[75] Manson. "The Teaching of Jesus." IX

[76] Meyer, Ben. "The church in Three tenses." p 11

[77] Manson. "Teachings of Jesus." pp 184-188

[78] Watts, James. "The Remnant theme." p 112

[79] Hasel. "Remnant" pp 40, 376, 402

[80] Jewell. "Election and Predestination, 34

[81] Watts. "Remnant." p 113

[82] Rowley. "The Biblical Doctrine of Election." 147-148

[83] Ibid. p 147

[84] Peter Richardson. "Israel in the Apostolic Church. p 10

[85] Ibid p. 203

[86] Ibid.
[87] B.F. Meyer. "Church in Three Tenses. p 36
[88] Meyer. Ibid p 127
[89] Christopher Rowland. "Christian Origins." p 152
[90] Watts. Remnant. p 117
[91] Sanders. "Jesus and Judaism. p 98

CHAPTER 3

DIASPORA: LATER DISPERSION

My Jewels

As promised, a discussion about a place where the actual word remnant doesn't appear, but does apply to the word. This example is found in Malachi 3:16, 17:

> "Then they that feared the Lord spake often one to another: and the Lord hearkened, and heard it, and a book of remembrance was written before him for them that feared the Lord, and that thought upon his name. And they shall be mine, saith the Lord of Hosts, in that day when I make up my jewels and I will spare them, as a man spareth his own son that serveth him."

Remnant is an important technical biblical term that is woven as a thread throughout the Old Testament and is found in the New Testament by name and also by alluding to the remnant theme. It is meant mainly for those (eschatological) faithful Jews who go through the final cleansing judgment. Their apocalyptic woes occur at the end time of the latter day Tribulation from which they will emerge victorious to enter with their king into the Millennium Kingdom.

The remnant is explicitly presented in other significant terms in the Bible. Some of these Bible passages do not contain the exact term itself, but remnant theology is revealed through related Bible concepts of the faithful remnant. One such passage to be looked at is Malachi 3:16-17.

In verse 16 there was a small group of the children of Israel who loved God and spoke about God when they were together. Going back to verse 13 in Malachi 3 we see the whole nation of Israel was rising up in anger and rebellion against the Lord. God says that these peoples' words were stout against him. The word for stout is used to describe battle scenes. There was a battle of words the people were engaged in with God. The word is the same word used in Exodus for how hardened in heart and obstinate Pharaoh was in his reactions towards God's plagues.

Verses 14 and 15 tell us that the rank and file Israelites had given up in service to God, they called it vanity, of no value. They turned off to and tuned out God and told Him that their hearts were not in it. God accepts that, but keeps trying, but they kept snubbing God and thinking they would avoid God's judgment.

Meantime, there were a few, an Israel within Israel, who feared the Lord and walked faithfully with him. God kept that in His mind as He observed those few who reverenced the Lord in their hearts and in their lives. The raucous crowd had works of wood, hay, and stubble, and God was rejecting them and was soon going to judge them. God knows what these people were doing all the time. He knows and is pleased with the small, faithful part of His people. God weeps over the sinners and He values His faithful. God will step in one day with judgment of these people. He will righteously judge His saints and hopefully with His promised return, good works and purity of heart as a spotless bride we may be.

Then in verse 17 God will claim His valuables. They include the godly saints in His church, but here in Malachi it is made up of the small amount of Israelites that have a heart for God and worship Him in spirit and in truth. So, the church is part of God's jewels. The faithful of Israel is seen here as making up "my jewels." The Hebrew word for jewels is *"Sehghullah,"* which gives jewels, possession, wealth, its meaning. What is the source of the word and where it came from is not known. It would be nice to think God Himself is the source.

The word, Seghulla, is a special word denoting God's own valuable possession. He has personally acquired, guided, and preserved the people of Israel.

> *"Now, therefore, if ye will obey my voice indeed, and keep my covenant, then ye shall be a peculiar treasure unto me above all people:"* (Exodus 19:5)

God had chosen them, brought them out of Egypt and molded them as the master potter into what he wanted them to be. God worked to bring them as a nation through all the fires, and gave Himself for them to redeem them out of iniquity;

> *"And purify unto himself a peculiar people, zealous of good works."* (Titus 2:14)

> *"But ye are a chosen generation, a royal priesthood, an holy nation, a peculiar people;"* (1 Peter 2:9a)

They were in a favored spot ever since God called them to be His chosen people. We as a church have a glorious calling. We that put our faith in Him become part of His body, the assembly of believers. Jews will still have the center of Christ's heart when they are called mid-tribulation. Consider God's proposal to Israel.

> *"Ye have seen what I did unto the Egyptians, and how I bare you on eagle's wings, and brought you unto myself. Now, therefore, if ye will obey my voice indeed, and keep my covenant, then ye shall be a peculiar treasure unto me above all people;"* (Exodus 19:4, 5)

They did not obey, and left God's protective guidance and were immediately put under law. However, God chose them to be His forever treasured possession. The Hebrew, Seghulla, is used early here, and seven more times in the Old Testament.

Again, Seghullah is used to refer to a royal treasure of gold and silver (Eccl. 2:8) and is used in reference to the Israelites.

> *"For the Lord hath chosen Jacob unto himself, and Israel for his peculiar treasure."* (Psalms 15:4)

Israel is God's special treasure, His possession, under His ownership, which He sets apart from all others of the world. In Malachi this treasure, or His jewels, are particular to the Jews of Israel.

> *"And I will spare them, as a man spareth his own son that serveth him."* (V. 17)

The end-time remnant that will be spared will make up the Israel redeemed by the Messiah. They will receive Him then, they will know who He is and at that point, all Israel shall be saved. When the

Lord sets up His Millennial Kingdom, all those who are His precious jewels, those who have feared the Lord and esteemed His name shall enter. The jewels of the kingdom are the Lord's, people not things. It is and will not be material possessions that are valuable to God, but if a people called out for Him are redeemed by His blood. The Lord will spare the remnant in that day of judgment. He will have compassion.

> *"In all their affliction he was afflicted,...in his love and in his pity he redeemed them:* (Isaiah 63.9)

Between Testaments

It was approximately 580 years after the Jews returned from Babylon until the Romans drove the Jews out of and destroyed the temple in Jerusalem in 70 A.D. The Jews had returned back to Israel due to God opening the Persian king's heart to allow them to go home.

It wasn't nearly four decades when sin and idolatry had again overtaken the Israelites. Over many years they had returned to harlotry and unfaithfulness, embraced Greek Hellenism, and their Jewish leaders became increasingly more corrupt. The Jews were ruled by high priests in an assembly set up to check their power and keep them in line. The assembly was known as the Sanhedrin. James Parkes, a Christian historian of Jewish life, in "A History of the Jewish People, wrote:

The history of the Jews is the story of a people inextricably interwoven with that of a religion. Neither can be told apart from the other. It is true that Jews would not have survived the long centuries of their total dispersion had there not been the cement of a religion molded to their need either to transform or to tolerate the condition of the corporate and individual lives...and in their dispersion their borrowings have been physical as well as intellectual and spiritual.

The Babylonian Captivity ended at the seventy year mark just as God had said. Babylon was badly defeated, a judgment of God, by the Persian Empire and King Cyrus allowed the Jews, with God's prompting, to return to Israel in 538 B.C. to rebuild the temple. The Jews enjoyed near 200 years of religious freedom and political self-government under the Persians.

In and around 333 B.C. Alexander the Great defeated the Persians and annexed Judea. The Jews did not suffer under Alexander as the same pattern of relations under the Persians was to reappear as a model under subsequent rulers through to the Romans and Moslems.

This meant that during these times leading up to the Diaspora, the Jewish people were for the most part conducting their own affairs and according to their own laws. The high priest and his assistants often had the favor of the imperial rulers behind them to enforce what they had commanded. This period of good relations between the Jews and whoever was in charge eventually led to the elevating of Judaism being an officially recognized and protected religion.

Jewish community came into focus with its center in the synagogue. This helped in shaping the self-governing aspect of Jewish life. This doesn't mean that the Jews had the run of the country. Alexander brought in Hellenism and all that its Greek civilization embodied.

After Alexander's death Palestine was ruled by Ptolemy of Egypt.

> *"And when he shall stand up, his kingdom shall be broken, and shall be divided toward the four winds of heaven;"* (Daniel 11:4a)

Alexander the Great died a drunk in 323 B.C. Four of his generals divided the empire into four regions. Ptolemy took Egypt to the south which ruled over the Jews in Palestine. He took many thousands of Jews to Egypt where they had full citizenship. The Greek culture dominated the Jews and their separation in Judaism suffered greatly. The Seleucid rulers of Asia defeated the Ptolemies and the new extra zealous Hellenizers formed a strong party among the Jews. Hellenization was so greatly strengthened that it threatened the very existence of Judaism.

There were two parties coming together among the Jews after 280 B.C. One was the Hellenizers who eventually became the Sadducees.

The Sadducees did not care much about their Judaism. They were worldly, intellectual, sophisticated, and they conformed to the world.[92] Later, in their ways, they shunned believing in anything spiritual. In the time of Christ they did not believe in miracles and the resurrection in bodily form. They Joined forces with their enemies, the Pharisees, to oppose the Lord Jesus Christ.

The Jewish party known as the anti-Hellenizers eventually became the Pharisees. They opposed anyone that was against traditional

Judaism and were very orthodox. In Christ's time they were proud, hypocritical, and instrumental in the death of Jesus. They turned Old Testament law into a weapon of unscriptural legalism and never presented a spiritual connotation to anything. They had the misguided zeal to enforce their ideas of religion over the people. They rejected the Lord Jesus for who He said He was. Jesus told His disciples to:

> *"Take heed and beware of the leaven of the Pharisees and of the Sadducees."* (Matthew 16:6).

> *"...He bade them not beware of the leaven of bread, but of the doctrine of the Pharisees and of the Sadducees."* (Matthew 16:12)

Further effects of Hellenism on the Jews at this time were upon Jewish religious thought and practice. Hellenism, being syncretistic in make-up, had borrowed from eastern religious thought. It may have been thought that it had been assimilated beforehand, and was transformative accordingly, all before being absorbed by Judaism.[93]

For whatever influenced the Hebrew mind in such a Hellenistically charged atmosphere, undoubtedly did the same in Gentile circles, just in a philosophic-religious way. The philosophy of Plato, the stoics, neo-pythagoreanism, and an element of orphic mystery-cult, were all contributing and corrupting Jewish thought.[94]

This is evident in the philosophy of "anthropological dualism," between the body and the soul, and spiritualization, by transforming religious tradition into popular superstitions through allegory and symbolism. In one place extra-biblical thought did have a profound effect on Judaism: in resurrection. More precise, in the resurrection of the body, which was Jewish dogma, but belief in the immortality of the spirit was Hellenistic.

Belief in the resurrection of the body, on the one hand, and in the immortality of the spirit, apart from the body, on the other, are not easy to reconcile outside of the Bible; but a compromise was achieved by postulating the existence of an intermediate state in which the body underwent a process of purification. The point here to be emphasized is that Greek influences played their part in the formulation of the Jewish doctrine of immortality.[95]

Around 200 B.C. the Ptolemies came to be under the Seleucid rules of Asia. Their jealous embracing of Hellenism affected Jewish life. The Seleucid ruler Antiochus Epiphanes ruled form 175-163 B.C. and wanted to wipe out the Jews. He was vile and terrorized the Jews as king of Syria. He is referred to as a little horn from Daniel 8:9. This horn is out of the third kingdom after Alexander left the scene. This little horn is the historical Antiochus Epiphanes, or Antiochus IV, the son of Antiochus the Great.

When Antiochus Epiphanes (the madman) attacked Jerusalem it was the Maccabees who opposed him. He brought an image of Jupiter into the Holy Temple of Jerusalem. This is the precedent, or the first abomination of desolation. He desecrated the altar with pig excrement and worshipped there.

> *"How long shall be the vision concerning the daily sacrifice, and the transgression of desolation,"* (Daniel 8:13)

Two supernatural beings are asking how long will this terrible abomination go on. This profanity of the temple is called the transgression of desolation.

> *"And he said unto me, unto two thousand and three hundred days, then shall the sanctuary be cleansed."* (Daniel 8:14)

This is between 6 and 7 years which is near the time that Antiochus Epiphanes executed his atrocities beginning or around 170 B.C. After that Judas Maccabeus ("The Hammer") defeated and expelled the Syrians from Jerusalem, and allowed the temple to be cleansed. The feast instituted as a result became known as the dedication of lights. The Jews were celebrating this day at the time of Christ and still do today. It is not mentioned in the Bible Canon because it was established in the time between the Testaments.

If by murdering, plundering, and burning his way through Jerusalem was a good plan for him, Antiochus was to get his come-uppance. His tyrannical ways finally woke up the Jews and that resulted in the Maccabean uprising. The priest Mattathias and his five sons slew the envoy of Antiochus, wrecked the heathen altar and then fled to the hills. They constantly attacked the Syrians and the Hellenist Jews who aided them. The next Sabbath the Orthodox Jews suffered a huge loss because they would not fight on the Sabbath and the slaughter was great. Mattathias convinced the

Orthodox that defending themselves even on the Sabbath would be acceptable.

As the revolt developed, a leader, Judas Maccabee, "The Hammer," was chosen. The ranks of Jews grew and together they defeated Syrian armies led by generals Ptolemaeus, Nicanor, and Gorgias in 166-165 B.C. Anthiochus was dead by 164 B.C.

Many battles and many leaders followed. The Maccabean struggle passed and the older Hellenists were discredited, but their ideology lived on in the party of the Sadducees. The Orthodox Maccabean line became the Pharisees of pre-Christian Judaism. As time passed, Hyrcanus II, who was the high priest, ascended to the throne in Jerusalem. His brother, Aristobulus, led an army of Sadducees and he became king in Jerusalem as well as high priest. However, Rome was threatening as Antipater, governor of Idumea, elevated himself which brought Pompey and his Roman legions on the scene. Roman rule over Palestine, including Jerusalem begins in 63 A.D. and Jewish independence ends.

The one-hundred-year period of Jewish independence was shattered when the Romans came to power and took over Palestine coming up against Aristobulus II, self-proclaimed king of Israel. Pompey, after three months of attacks against Jerusalem, entered the city after killing 12,000 Jews. Although Pompey and his men entered the Temple, he declined to desecrate anything and allowed Temple worship to continue. After the death of Julius Caesar, Herod was appointed by Caesar Augustus to be tetrarch of

Galilee and Perea and ruled for forty-two years. Antipas was the youngest son of Herod the Great, and after his brother, Aristobulus, was executed, and his oldest brother convicted of attempted poisoning of Herod the Great, the father, Antipas became the heir and was put in power around 4 B.C.

With the death of Herod the Great, the father, in 4 B.C. which was not even celebrated, the time between the Testaments, comes to an end. There were some notable things that stand out from this time. From the end of the book of Malachi to when the New Testament begins, again there is a 400-year gap which some call the 400 silent years. They are silent because God sent no prophets to the nation of Israel, and the Canon of the Holy Scripture was being given out of the mouth of God.

During this time there arose groups or parties, of which the Pharisees and Sadducees were already mentioned. The Pharisees were more sympathetic with the procurator of the regime. The Sadducees were the party of the Jerusalem aristocracy and the High Priesthood. Where the Pharisees were open to making disciples to themselves, the Sadducees were a closed party. They formally opposed each other in many ways.

Scribes

From the days of Ezra came the Scribes, the group that held up the law and expounded from it. You could say they upheld the letter of the law as opposed to the spirit of the law. They cared not for the Messiah, they only knew where He was to be born. The Scribes possessed great head knowledge, but it didn't necessarily translate to their actual lives. We all need a fundamental learning of the Bible and all of its theological truth contained within, but we must allow it to take hold of our hearts. The scribes would dwell on and hammer home some point of law where most people would put up a stonewall defense against.

Herodians

These were the political opportunists. They wanted the favor and access to the power of the throne through Herod. They were Jews of influence and standing, and would be continuously appeasing the power on the throne seeking political favors. They were also very friendly towards the Romans.

Zealots

The Zealots were at the opposite end of the political spectrum from the Herodians. Where the Herodians were great appeasers to Rome, the Zealots despised and resisted Rome at every turn. They continuously tried to incite fellow Jews of Judea to rise up in revolt against the Roman Empire and throw them out of the Holy Land.

The Essenes

The Essenes are a group that is popularized today due to popularity of the Dead Sea Scrolls. The Essenes and the Pharisees have their roots in the Orthodox leaders of Maccabean times who once stood against the Hellenists. They were a more extreme reaction to the corruptions of Jewish life that were prevalent then. They had a form of monastic existence in separate communities, such as at their headquarters of Qumran. According to what is scarcely known about them, they were somewhat divided when it comes to marriage and women, with one part of them that indulged in such activities, and another of an order of marrying Essenes.

Members of the Essene community studied Scripture, but had no use for the doctrines of inspiration or preservation of the words of God. They had other religious books besides the scrolls of Scripture. They shared work in order to be self-sufficient. They were anti-slavery and anti-war. Their Essene colonies were small in number, and all tolled there may have been about 4,000 Essenes in total. Early on they were repulsed by the corruptions in pre-Christian Judaism. This led to most of the Essene members to withdraw Jewish community life to set up their own communes.

They became very pious and considered themselves the only true, pure Israel refusing to partake with self-perceived views of what they believed as corrupt religious ceremonies at the Jerusalem Temple. Everyone who writes about the Esssenes stresses the strictness of Essene discipline and rigidity by which the law was enforced by them.

The Dead Sea Scrolls are attributed to the Essenes as having been written by them. They are not very useful to the saint and cannot be relied on as the truth. It is not known if the Essenes had authentic Hebrew (Masoretic) manuscripts to copy from, and if they did, where are they? Besides, their technique of copying cannot be relied upon as being anywhere close to the Masoretic Jews.

They ended up making the law a burden instead of a blessing. It was also lawful to do good on the Sabbath, and the temple services themselves were never repudiated by Christ. Christianity was not an ascetic or monastic movement, and both the Pharisees and the Essenes ended up rejecting the Lord.

The Apocrypha

The Apocrypha was written in this era as a collection of ancient Jewish writings from about 250 B.C. on. These books have come to be accepted as inspired scripture in the theology of the Roman Catholic Church. The Protestant and Jewish view of the Apocrypha is that they bear no marks of inspiration and do not belong in the Canon. It is used, sometimes, for the information it has contained within on the life and thought of pre-Christian Judaism. Once again, it is rejected on the grounds that it is not inspired, and the Lord and his Apostles never used it and never referred to it at all.

The word itself is from the Greek, *abscondita*, which means hidden and refers to writings which have obscure origins or which were heretical.

The term Apocrypha is applied to fifteen books which are added to Roman Catholic Bibles but rejected by non-Catholics. They were written from about 250 B.C. to about 100 A.D. The Council of Trent in 1546 demanded that the Apocrypha be accepted as sacred and canonical in their entirety or have anathema (death) pronounced upon them. By placing unwritten traditions of the R.C. church on an equal par as the Holy Scriptures, was to make the Holy Scriptures impotent and cut off the reformation at the knees. That meant if only the sixty-six books of the King James Bible are referred to as expressing the supreme will of God would be considered useless in their church.[96]

There are at least fifteen reasons the Apocrypha are rejected by Christians.[97] Quoting from the Encyclopedia by Dr. Cloud, is the first reason: they are not included in the original Hebrew O.T. preserved by the Jews. Romans 3:1, 2 states that God used the Jews to preserve His word; therefore, we know that He guided them in the rejection of the Apocryphal books from the canon of scripture.[98]

Readers familiar with readings in the Apocrypha feel that the Apocryphal books show a lower level of writing quality of content than Canonical Scriptures do. They are filled with geographical and historical inaccuracies. Simply, they do not measure up to what is in the sixty-six accepted books of the Bible. None of the material in the Apocrypha was quoted by either Jesus Christ or the Apostles, where every part of the Old Testament was. There is magic being taught in their words, angels are everywhere and interacting with humans, and the heresy that dead saints are interceding for humans on earth.

Yes, the Apocryphal books are found in King James Bibles within the first thirty years of printing them in the 1600s. They were promptly removed. However, they were all in one group and inserted in between the Old Testament and the New Testament. They were never dispersed between the books of the Old Testament, as they are found in Roman Catholic Bibles of today. It is true that some of the books of the Apocrypha possess some historical value, especially about the silent years between the testaments, by no means must they be given place or be considered on the same level as Holy Scripture. Think of them as being on the same par as the historian Josephus or any other similar type of writer of that time.

There were other books and collections written during this time, for example, the Pseudepigrapha. These were a number of books which varied in quality and character. Among these books are: Book of Enoch, Book of Jubilees, Testaments of the XII Patriarch, Testament or Assumption of Moses, the Psalms of Solomon, and Apocalypse of Baruch. It is said that along with the Old Testament and Apocrypha, the Jewish Pseudepigrapha had a definite influence on the language and ideas of the New Testament. Questionably, some sayings and proverbs occur which supposedly match with those used by Jesus. This is highly questionable and a bit over the top. It may be useful to know that some of the Pseudepigrapha issued supposedly from groups of a similar type as those of the Qumran community.[99] They have found fragments of four of the five divisions of "Enoch" in caves, of some ten Hebrew copies of Jubilees, and Hebrew text of the "Testament of Naphtali."[100]

Dead Sea Scrolls

The site where the scrolls were found and which has been excavated shows an occupation by a semi-monastic group (Essenes) to be around 100 B.C. There was a break in the settlement because of the earthquake in 31 B.C., with the resumption starting near the Christian era until the destruction of the settlement together with the sect during the war with Rome A.D. 67-73.

They discovered the scrolls starting in 1947 thru to 1956, in caves northwest of the Dead Sea and 13 miles southeast of Jerusalem. Because the caves are in extremely dry conditions 1300 feet below sea level, the Dead Sea Scrolls were preserved to a high degree. There are about 900 different writings and seem to have been written between 250 B.C. and 68 A.D. The condition of the scrolls is good even with the majority of them being in fragments. Most of the writings are on sheep or goat skins, some on papyrus and clay, and there are two written on copper. Every book of the Old Testament is represented in writing except for the book of Esther.

The Dead Sea Scrolls merely confirm that in nearly all places that the preserved Masoretic text of the Old Testament is proven reliable. There is absolutely no reason to doubt that what God has preserved is true down to the jots and titles. There is no reason then for any reliance on any fragments of so-called scripture written by a weird, questionable cult.

Silence of God Ending

One more change that was affected since the return from Babylon was the change of the Jewish High Priests from religious leaders to political leaders. They gained and exercised great control over the Jewish population. They started and grew from Zerubbabel (Nehemiah 12). The governments over the Jews during the silent years entrusted the high priest and his cohorts with ruling over the Jewish people, and hence became the priestly rule as well as religious leaders. The high priest line traced from Jeshua, who came up with Jerubbabel from Babylon during the first return. This is the same priest in Zechariah's vision, Chapter 3.

> *"And he shewed me Joshua (Jeshua) the high priest standing before the angel of the Lord, and Stan standing at his right hand to resist him."* (Zechariah 3:1)

The line continues through Zorakim, Eliashib, Joida, Jonathan to Jadda, the latest mentioned character (historical) in the Old Testament.

From about the last five centuries before Christ, four distinct developing aspects of Jewish life are seen to emerge.

There was first a desire and a drive to emphasize the daily sacrifice and ceremony that surrounded temple life. There was intense organizing of the ceremonies and offerings by the people as well as for High Feast Days, such as the Day of Atonement. This gave deep roots and dependence upon the priesthood and the temple as center points for Judaism and Jewish life. Having the Jewish faithful carry out ceremonial religious procedures maintained unity and continuity in the Jewish Community.

Second, there was an increase in legalism in Jewish religious life. Having more and more synagogues in place, the Jewish Torah became increasingly important to the nation. As the population of Israel radiated out from Jerusalem, the people needed to be connected to temple worship, etc., and did this by attending Synagogues for Sabbath days. The Torah itself, that is the

Pentateuch became central to religious life. It was taught on, memorized, given interpretation, reverenced. So, the word of God offered a sense of continuity of Jewish life.

Thirdly, was the development of a philosophy of life. This changed on its way out of Egypt, through Greece, and picked up some aspects from Rome and Israel. These were mostly in the form of wise sayings of the ages and sages, compiled into recommendations for prosperity and happiness in life. During these late centuries before Christ, the collections of Israel's wisdom-precepts had formed, and these were forged in the fires of experience into go-to philosophies for life. What stood out in practice during this time was the ageless retribution and reward way of life. It was accepted that a life of good works and well-doing must bring ample reward, while evil had to always be punished. The book of Job and its contents made a challenge to this belief, but with overwhelming agreement of philosophy it was added as another link of continuing in Jewish life.

Lastly, as a recovery for lost hope, eschatological, or end-time things gave support to the Jews in their dark days. They would hope, and that led to the belief that God would soon intervene in man's affairs to their benefit. Eventually, with all things considered, God would visit judgment on the Jews' enemies and bring vindication to His people. The prospect of deliverance from their enemies through prophecy, the soon coming of the Messiah, and the impending day of the Lord, were all familiar themes to the Jewish people. The people were eventually dazzled by all the prophetic buzzers and bells. Numbers, figures, over-used and too detailed interpretations, had peoples' minds railroaded into love for the sensational and not for the truth. The Jews, believed not that God was ready to move, therefore His intervention could not be far off. Their forward looking hope of restoration as a free, Godly nation, was their outlook and a uniting continuity in their life.

Therefore, the Jewish nation had the four forces of sacramentalism, legalism, religious philosophy, and apocalypticism, all acting together to unify Jewish life. They had to stick to belief in God through temple rites, ordering their lives according to the law, applying spiritual and worldly wisdom to understand God, and studying writings of an eschatological nature related to the Lord's Kingdom; all went well. All the activities became too mechanical. It brought the people close together, but there was a shutting off of the main purpose for which God chose them as His chosen people. They ceased to be that shining beacon of light, shining bright God's salvation on a dark world. They had all the spiritual tools: The temple where they could meet God, the law given by God, wisdom that came from their priests, and a hope for the future kingdom, but grew hard of heart and cold towards their Father in heaven. Despite what was taught in their Judaism, and their rich history of their fathers, Israel fell short of their mission and calling of God. They clung to earthly things, were misled by man-made ordinances, and completely veered off track of their heavenly destiny.

Israel had failed and was failing. God and His purpose did not fail, God never fails. God shut down the light and the prophesies to the Jews for 400 years. He would send forth His Son to reclaim whatever remnant of the Israelites that would turn to Him, and bring deliverance to a lost world.

Christ would be sent to the world. The Jews, the Greeks, the Romans, the people of the Orient, were all part of God's preparation for the provision of salvation. This was the fulfillment of the fullness of time, in which the Saviour would appear.

> *"But when the fulness of time was come, God sent forth his Son, made of a woman, made under the law,"* (Galatians 4:4)

Preparations

The events of the times between the Testaments, the 400 years, were leading up to and setting the stage for Christ to come as light into the darkness of the world. Pagans around the world at that time were dissatisfied with their beliefs in polytheism and mythologies, especially the Greeks and the Romans. They were gradually being drawn to the Hebrew Scriptures, easily accessible in their languages. The Jews were very low, being under the Romans and strictly held in abeyance under the Jewish priests. Their Judaism was being more and more polluted by religious/political sects such as the Pharisees and Sadducees. The people of Israel, being in somewhat dire straits were looking for a way out from under. In their hearts this could only happen with the appearance of the Messiah.

They had some advantage for that time. There were built modern roads, for that time, that connected trade and service centers. These could be used in the spreading of the gospel. There was a common language spoken at the time; *Koine* Greek, the language of the New Testament. On top of all this, the Romans had granted a modicum of peace and free rein to travel. The 400 years of silence in the years between the Old and the New Testaments, were about to be shattered by a beacon of light from heaven, by the Lord Jesus Christ, the Son of God, and His gospel.

Prophecies

It was known for a very long time, since Adam and Eve, that there would be a Saviour to redeem mankind after the fall. Eve had just been tempted by Satan and sinned against God, and Adam and all mankind went down in the fall. A fallen nature and the propensity to always sin was the norm. Eternal damnation was the grim outlook for all humans, total darkness and irreversible separation from God was the sentence. God had planned a perfect creation for a perfect man made in His image.

God said, "and I will put enmity between thee and the woman, and between thy seed and her seed; it shall bruise they head, and thou shalt bruise his heel." (Genesis 3:15). "...God sent forth his son, made of a woman... (Galatians 4:4)

It was prophesied that Christ would be born of a virgin:

> *"Behold, a virgin shall conceive, and bear a son, and shall call his name Immanuel."* (Isaiah 7:14)

> *"Behold, a virgin shall be with child, and shall bring forth a son, and they shall call his name Immanuel."* (Matthew 1:23)

Christ's deity was confirmed by Scripture:

"For unto us a child was born, unto us a son is given: and the government shall be upon his shoulder: and his name shall be called wonderful, counsellor, the mighty God, the everlasting Father, the Prince of Peace.": (Isaiah 9:6)

Jesus Christ, as the Son of God came to fulfill the Old Testament.

"Think not that I am come to destroy the law, or the prophets: I am not come destroy, but to fulfill." (Matthew 5:17)

"Also I will make him my first-born, higher than the kings of the earth." (Psalm 89:27)

Jesus Christ is King

"And the Lord shall be king over all the earth: In that day shall there be one Lord, and his name one." (Zechariah 14:9)

"behold, they king cometh unto thee: he is just, and having salvation; lowly, and riding upon an ass, and upon a colt the foal of an ass." (Zechariah 9:9)

Genealogy

The genealogy of Jesus Christ opens the New Testament at the beginning of the gospel of Matthew (Matthew 1-17). It breaks down into three sections:

1. It starts with Abraham to David, 1-6.
2. From Solomon up to the Babylonian captivity, 7-11.
3. Then it goes from the Babylonian captivity to Joseph, the stepfather, 12-17)

This shows that the supernatural Saviour's earthy, human line proceeds from Abraham, which places the Lord in the nation of Israel. The line from David puts Christ in the line of royalty and on the throne of David. Jesus, as Messiah, will be the One who will rule the nations with a rod of iron, and has God as His father. King Messiah is able to declare that the God of Israel is His Father.

> *"I will declare the decree: the Lord hath said unto me, thou art my son; this day have I begotten thee."* (Psalm 2:7)

The New Testament, by opening with the genealogy of the Lord Jesus shows that He is the Messiah. He is the Son of David through Solomon to Rehoboam to Zerubbabel. This is the true messianic line which makes Jesus Christ able to be King of Israel. He is the Son of God directly, since Joseph was His adopted father, and He is the son of God through the virgin birth.

> *"Now the birth of Jesus Christ was on this wise; when as his mother Mary was espoused to Joseph, before they came together, she was found with child of the Holy Ghost.* (Matthew 1:18)

> *"...for that which is conceived in her is of the Holy Ghost."* (Matthew 1:20)

Only as the Son and heir of David could the Lord Jesus Christ be proven the Messiah. This much is known from the genealogy in Matthew that Christ Jesus is the Son and heir of David, where in the genealogy found in the gospel of Luke we have given the direct, human descent of Jesus from David. Since both genealogies trace Jesus to David, they together emphasize His rightful claim to be heir to the throne of David. In Jewish genealogy an heir would make their claim through the father. His right to the throne of David comes through Joseph, His adoptive father.[101] The genealogy found in Luke traces the Lord Jesus through Mary to Adam, "connecting Christ with the predicted seed of the woman (Genesis 3:15).[102]

> *"And I will put enmity between three and the woman, and between thy seed and her seed:"* (Genesis 3:15)

Jesus Christ was born in the line of Abraham and in the line of David. Jesus Christ is the fulfillment of everything said in the Old Testament. Genealogies were very important in Israel. They were meticulously kept records which were used to establish legitimate claims to be who one said they were. These were important when the Jews returned from Babylon in order to check and see who were in the priestly line.

> *"These sought their register among those that were reckoned by genealogy, but they were not found: therefore were they, as polluted, put from the priesthood."* (Ezra 2:62)

The Pharisees and the priests never questioned the Lord Jesus' genealogy.

> *"The book of the generations of Jesus Christ, the son of David, the son of Abraham.* (Matthew 1:1)

What does it mean the book of the generation of Jesus Christ? This is important for we find a second book in Genesis 5:1)

> *"This is the book of the generations of Adam."* (Genesis 5:1)

Adam was the first human created by God. He was the head of the human family and the one we all inherited the sin nature from. To get into the family Adam, the family human, all one has to do is be born of a human mother here on earth. We all get in by the simple fact of birth. The problem is that through Adam we are all born to die and go to hell.

> *"Wherefore, as by one man sin entered into the world, and death by sin; and so death passed upon all men,"* (Romans 5:12)

To get cleansed and go from death to life, we have to get into the book of the Lord Jesus Christ. The entering into that like takes another birth, a rebirth. There must be a new birth.

> *"Verily, verily, I say unto thee, except a man be born again, he cannot see the kingdom of God.* (John 3:3)

Being in the first book of Adam is shared by everyone who has ever lived and died. What is important in this life is that a man be born again to get written into the Lamb's book of life. That must be done now, before this world is ended, there are no do-overs.

> *"The son of David, the son of Abraham."* (Mt. 1:1)

It is important to see here that the Holy Spirit moves Matthew to write son of David before son of Abraham. This is all about the kingly line producing the Messiah, and here Matthew puts it in this order to make clear that Jesus Christ is indeed the Messiah. There is no mistake about that.

Matthew presents Jesus Christ as the promised Messiah, the One who will establish the kingdom of heaven on earth. He must be in this kingly linen of David in the fulfillment of all the prophesies made to David.

Christ is also the son of Abraham and that is just as important. That makes a huge difference after what God said to Abraham, "and in thy seed shall all the nations of the earth be blessed; because thou hast obeyed my voice." (Genesis 22:18)

> *"Now to Abraham and his seed were the promises made. He saith not, And to seeds, as of many, but as of one, And to thy seed, which is Christ."* (Galatians 3:16)

Just as true then is that Jesus Christ is the son of Abraham.

Matthew 1 Verse 11 says:

> *"And Josias begat Jechonias and his brethren, about the time they were carried away to Babylon:"*

In this verse Jehoiakim is skipped but it includes Jechonias. God had told Jechonias that none of his seed would sit on the throne.

> *"As I live saith the Lord, through Coniah (minus the Je) the son of Jehoiakim king of Judah were the signet… Write ye this man childless,…for no man of his seed shall prosper sitting upon the throne of David, and ruling any more in Judah."* (Jeremiah 22: 24, 30)

It was the result of grievous sin that God judged Jechonias and cursed his seed to be never in line for David's throne. This is in Joseph's line, but

Joseph is not the father of Jesus. Joseph gave to Jesus the legal title to the throne of David since Joseph, being the husband of Mary who bore the Lord Jesus. Jesus is not the seed of Joseph or Jeconiah. Both Joseph and Mary were from the line of David through the two different lines of two different sons of David.

We know that Christ Jesus was truly the Son of God through the virgin birth. What the curse of Jeconiah showed in the Old Testament, was that it would be impossible for the coming Messiah to have a natural father. The Lord Jesus' father was God. Again:

> "I will declare the decree: the Lord hath said unto me, Thou art my son; this day have I begotten thee." (Psalm 2:7)

The birth of the Messiah pushed aside the old curse of Jecohiah, and allowed Jesus Christ to be entitled to the throne. As King David lay dying, he brought the charge to Solomon to keep on the path in all the ways of obedience. He was to walk as David had before him, in all his heart to keep God's statutes, commandments, judgments, and his testimonies. Why the conditions?

> "That the Lord may continue his word which he spake concerning me, saying, if thy children take heed to their way, to walk before me in truth with all their heart and with all their soul, there shall not fail thee (said he) a man on the throne of Israel." (1 Kings 2:4)

> "If thy children will keep my covenant and my testimony that I shall teach them, their children shall also sit upon thy throne for evermore" (Psalm 132:12)

The failure of the kingly line from King Solomon on was due to disobedience to all the commands of the Lord. The kings were supposed to set a higher standard as they represented the Lord on earth. Due to this failure, God was free to send His Son, the Lord Jesus Christ, to fulfill His promise for David's seed to sit upon the throne. Jesus was born of a virgin, from the line of David through Nathan, therefore fulfilling the covenant to David through the virgin birth.

Returning to the Old Testament prophesies of our Lord Jesus Christ, it needs to be noted that He is the only person who has fulfilled all the messianic prophecy. That alone establishes the messianic credentials of the Lord Jesus Christ. No one alive or dead can lay claim to fulfilling of the prophesies about Jesus, no one.

Peter Stoner, in his classic book "Science Speaks," calculated the chance of any man fulfilling these prophesies, even down to the present time, to be 1 in 100,000,000,000,000,000 (10 to the 17th power).[103]

To list a few fulfillments of prophecy, we know Jesus was born in Bethlehem, John the Baptist went before Him, he entered Jerusalem on a donkey, was betrayed by a friend (Judas) for thirty pieces of silver, was humble and silent before His accusers, died by the Roman Crucifixion, having His hands and feet nailed to the cross.

In addition to the real presence of Jesus as the Angel of the Lord, J. Barton Payne listed some 574 verses in the Old Testament that had direct personal messianic fore-telling. Payne found 127 personal messianic predictions involving some 348 verses that had any or all types of real and typological prophesies of Jesus' first or second coming.[104] A few more predictions or prophecies appear in the Pentateuch.

> *"God shall enlarge Japheth, and he shall dwell in the Tents of Shem: and Canaan shall be his servant."* (Genesis 9:27)

> *"And I will make of thee a great nation, and I will bless thee, and make thy name great; and thou shalt be a blessing:"* (Genesis 12:2)

> *"The scepter shall not depart from Judah, nor a lawgiver from between his feet, until Shiloh come; and unto him shall the gathering of the people be."* (Genesis 49:10)

> *"I shall see him, but not now: I shall behold him, but not nigh: there shall come a star out of Jacob, and a scepter shall rise out of Israel,"* (Numbers 24:17)

> *"The Lord thy God will raise up unto thee a prophet from the midst of thee, of thy brethren, like unto me; unto him ye shall hearken;"* (Deuteronomy 18:15)

We have then in Gen. 9:27, God coming to live/dwell in the tents of Shem, who are the Semite people. God then chose Abram from the Semite people, and He was going to be a blessing for all the nations in Genesis 12:3. The scepter of ruling was given to Judah, the fourth son, and from the tribe of Judah is where the line of the Messiah would descend (Gen. 49: 8-12). That is the meaning of the "Star out of Jacob," the ruler that rises out of Israel. The word prophet in Deuteronomy 18:15 is the Messiah that would come to be of the nation of Israel.

There can be found the coming Messiah in the book of Job.

> *"If there be a messenger with him, an interpreter, one among a thousand, to shew unto man his uprightness:"* (Job 33:23)

God called the Lord Jesus a faithful priest to whom it will be to do all that is in the heart and mind of God.

> *"And I will raise me up a faithful priest,"* (1 Samuel 3:35)

The coming Messiah is said to be rejected.

> *"The stone which the builders refused is become the headstone of the corner."* (Psalm 118:24)

The Messiah would be reviled in His very house of Israel.

> *"For the zeal of thine house hath eaten me up; and the reproaches of them that reproached thee are fallen upon me*: (Psalm 69:9)

The Lord God who sent His Son will behold Him die on the cross and will have to turn from Him as He is made sin to die for us. This is told to take place long into the future.

> *"My God, my God, why hast thou forsaken me? Why art thou so far from helping me, and form the words of my roaring?"* (Psalm 22:1)

After being sacrificed on the cross and killed, the Lord Jesus will be resurrected and be alive.

> *"Thou wilt show me a path of life: in thy presence is fullness of joy; at thy right hand there are pleasures for evermore."* (Psalm 16:11)

God will send His Son, the Messiah, the Lord Jesus Christ to be conqueror and ruler.

> *"The Lord shall send the rod of thy strength out of Zion: rule thou in the midst of thine enemies.* (Psalm 110:2)

The Lord shall scatter His enemies and He shall be triumphant and be their king.

> *"Let God arise, let his enemies be scattered: let them also that hate him flee before him."* (Psalm 68:1)

It was prophesied that the Messiah would be born in Bethlehem.

> *"But thou, Bethlehem Ephratah, though thou be little among the thousands of Judah, yet out of thee shall he come forth unto me that is to be ruler in Israel; whose goings forth have been from of old, from everlasting."* (Micah 5:2)

Its already been shown that Messiah, Christ Jesus, was born of a virgin (Isaiah 7:14). It was also prophesied that John the Baptist would go before him, preparing the way and announcing the Saviour (Isaiah 40: 3-5, Malachi 3:1). Zechariah says in Zech. 9:9 that the king and a prophet of Nazareth had come, and fulfilled Matthew 21:8-11). In about a week after entering Jerusalem the Messiah would be betrayed by Judas (Psalm 69:25), fulfilled in Acts 1:20.

These are only some of the hundreds of prophesies of the coming of the Messiah, the Lord Jesus Christ. It is also prophesied that Jesus would return a second time to earth (Daniel 7:13). The Old Testament would pinpoint exactly that the Messiah, in the person of Jesus Christ, would rule

His kingdom in the city of Jerusalem as King of Kings, and the nations would say:

> "Come ye, and let us go up to the mountain of the Lord, to the house of the God of Jacob; and he will teach us of his ways," (Isaiah 2:3)

For all of the Scriptures full of prophesies, the Jews should have been prepared for their Messiah, their Saviour. They were caught unawares mostly, guilty of looking the other way, being totally unprepared. They should have known who their Messiah was, but did not. How could they? When Christ was born it was in the evil days of Herod the King, a self-centered, idiot of a man. The men from the east arrived ready to worship Christ Jesus, for they had believed the prophecies and knew exactly who was come to earth.

Herod, when he heard that there was another king just born, one that would challenge him, sought out from the chief priests and scribes where Christ was born.

> "And they said unto him, in Bethlehem of Judea: for thus it is written by the prophet." (Matt. 2-5)

They then proceeded to quote Micah 5:2 to King Herod. He sent the easterners off and awaited the news. But they never returned, being warned of an angel and Herod sought to kill every child under the age of two. This fulfilled Jeremiah's prophecy of 31:15. Herod died and they brought Jesus out from protection in Egypt, which fulfilled the prophecy that Jesus should be called a Nazarene (Isa. 11:1; Jer. 23:5). In Christ's family making their home in

Nazareth, the prophecy of Isaiah was fulfilled, Christ being the young branch of the royal family of David.[105]

Nearly 40 years after the death of Christ, when the nation of Israel was destroyed, it was assured that no one else could claim the title of Messiah of Israel. The genealogy for the Messiah went from David to Solomon to Rehoboam to Jeconiah to Zerubbabel. All the records were destroyed with Israel, Jerusalem, and the Temple, of the proof of the genealogy and the link to Rehoboam was concluded. The order of proof right now would be a trace of the Davidic line back to Zerubbabel, and also be virgin born. Then this would-be imposter Messiah must be seen coming with the clouds of heaven to set up an everlasting kingdom.

The only true genealogy of the true Messiah is David to Solomon to Rehoboam to Jeconiah to Zerubbabel to Jesus of Nazareth. Only Jesus Christ of Nazareth can be Messiah and King.

Diaspora

The Diaspora is the term given to the dispersions of Israel that have occurred loosely from 722 B.C. up to 70-135 A.D. It began with the Assyrians invading and capturing the northern kingdom of Israel in 722 B.C. to the defeat and captivity of Judah in 586 B.C.[106] It was the Persians that granted in a decree that the Jews could return to their home. Many did not and had colonies in Persia and throughout the Mediterranean and Mesopotamian areas. By the time of Jesus a very large number of Jews lived outside of Israel.

212

A more up to date version of Jewish Diaspora is what it means; a scattering, to scatter. It is true that the Jews were a scattered people when James addressed them.

> *"James, a servant of God and of the Lord Jesus Christ, to the twelve tribes which are scattered abroad,"* (James 1:1)

Paul wrote of the scattered tribes, some of which he scattered himself; "Unto which promise our twelve tribes, instantly serving God day and night, hope to come." (Acts 26:7). The Jews were left wondering when Jesus told the Jews that where He would go they could not come. They were befuddled and wondering if the Lord; "will he go unto the dispersed among the Gentiles, and teach the Gentiles?' (John 7:35). Peter was more specific about where they were: "Peter, an apostle of Jesus Christ, to the strangers scattered throughout Pontus Galatia, Cappadocia, Asia, and Bithynia," (1 Peter 1:1). These were elect; according to the foreknowledge of God the Father, and Jesus Christ, and the sanctification of the Spirit.

At the time of Pentecost, the beginning of the church;

> *"There were dwelling at Jerusalem Jews, devout men, out of every nation under heaven."* (Acts 2:5)

Then, at that time did the power of the Holy Spirit fill the house where the 120 believers were, and they were all filled with the Holy Spirit and spoke in all the native languages of all that were gathered in Jerusalem. They were, according to Scripture, confounded, "because that every man heard them speak in his own language. (Acts 2:6) These were the believing ones and they all returned to their home countries with the salvation message. Not all believed, especially the chief priests' and scribes' disciples, which were most of the population;" Others mocking said, "these men are full of new wine." (Acts 2:13)

The main meaning of Diaspora today of the Jews came in 70 A.D., with the destruction of the Temple and Jerusalem. The Jews will be cast out of their land, a second time, and scattered throughout the nations for 1900 years. Then, the nation of Israel in the modern, latter days was reborn in 1948.

With all the light provided by Christ the Creator in the world, up to His death in the early 30's A.D., coupled with the light of the Holy Spirit, what was the spiritual problem of Israel? How did it lead to their blindness to where they couldn't even recognize their Messiah when they came eye to eye with each other?

A judged blindness had descended upon Israel long ago as disclosed by Isaiah:

"...go and tell this people, hear ye indeed, but understand not; and see ye indeed, but perceive not." (Isaiah 7:9)

"...and shut their eyes; lest they see with their eyes, and hear with their ears, and understand with their heart," (Isaiah 7:10)

In Matthew 13:13-15, the Lord is responding to the Apostles' question about why He spoke to the Jews in parables. Jesus answered them that they do not see, hear, or understand spiritual matters. It was Satan who blinded them that they could not see.

> "In whom the god of this world hath blinded the minds of them which believe not, lest the light of the glorious gospel of Christ, who is the image of God, should shine unto them." (2 Corinthians 4:4)

The Jews were in open rebellion against the Lord Jesus and later the Apostles. They could see, but they refused to see. They could hear, but refused to hear. They could very well understand, but refused to accept the truth. They would rather hold on to old religious traditions instead of walking in the light.

In Isaiah 6:9, the Lord tells the people that their hearts are made fat. The Greek for make fat is, *pachuno*, and it means stupid, insensible, inattentive, dull, and callous. We all know what stupid is, a lack of intelligence or reason. Insensitive is incapable of feeling, no life or spirit; spiritually dead. Inattentive is not paying attention, disregarding. This is a bad position to be in, especially when it comes to God, who is always trying to get our attention. Being dull of hearing is not hearing clearly, for example, it goes in one ear and comes out totally opposite. Being callous is being hardened in heart, feeling no sympathy for others. The Pharisees, Sadducees, and chief priests and scribes, and all the other non-saved Jews sadly were all of these. These people got this way gradually, little by little until they reached the point past caring about putting any effort into a vigorous obedience to truth and righteousness.

Matthew 13:15 says,

"...lest at any time they should see with their eyes...and should understand with their heart, and should be converted."

The Greek word for heart is, *kardia,* used in the Bible as the control over our thoughts, reasonings, and understanding, will, judgment, affections, love, hate, and the whole gamut of emotions. These things affect one's physical heart if they are not right or in line with God and His words. It is used as a metonym for the mind in general. This part of us is so important to be close to God in all his ways or end up like the unsaved one's in Christ's time.

...and should be converted, the Lord says. Converted comes from the Greek, *epistrepho*, meaning to turn, turn to or towards, turn to God and holiness. The Lord is waiting for conversion, it didn't happen with these spiritually dead Jews, but He will never give up even in our present day. To convert means to change direction, have a new walk with Christ.

"The law of the Lord is perfect, converting the soul: the testimony of the Lord is sure, making wise the simple." (Psalm 19:7)

The Lord Jesus spoke in parables to explain spiritual truths, but the Pharisees, etc. had already rejected Jesus because they did not have divinely illuminated minds to handle the truth. There would be no amount of explanation to make them understand.

"But the natural man receiveth not the things of the Spirit of God: for they are foolishness

unto him: neither can he know them, because they are spiritually discerned." (1 Corinthians 2:14).

The Pharisees, etc, could look at and hear Jesus with physical eyes and ears, but there was no capability to understand the truth because of their rejection of him.

"But if our gospel be hid, it is hid to them that are lost:" (2 Corinthians 4:3)

To the saved and elect, Jesus said:

"Unto you it is given to know the mysteries of the kingdom of God: but to others in parables; that seeing they might not see, and hearing they might not understand." (Luke 8:10)

So, in the Old Testament it was foretold this blindness would appear in Israel when their Messiah was come. It came upon them as anticipated and was the cause of national Israel to reject their Messiah.

"Ye men of Israel, hear these words; Jesus of Nazareth, a man approved of God among you by miracles and wonders and signs, which God did by him in the midst of you, as ye yourselves also know:

Him being delivered by the determinate counsel and foreknowledge of God, ye have taken, and by wicked hands have crucified and slain:" (Acts 2:22, 23)

This blindness had the unfortunate occasion of the breaking off of the natural (Jewish) branches of the olive tree.

"Well, because of unbelief they were broken off, and thou standest by faith." (Romans 11:20)

They would not believe that Jesus Christ was the Messiah.

"What then? Israel hath not obtained that which he seeketh for; but the election hath obtained it, and the rest were blinded." (Romans 11:7)

Right here Paul states Israel's spiritual condition. Israel was a country of seekers. The work seek is from the Greek, *epizeteo*, and describes seeking to acquire or obtain something, strive after, long for earnestly. There is an element of persistence to the Israelites seeking after righteousness, but failing due to going about it by works. Israel, as a nation, did not attain the blessing they sought, but the chosen portion of them had obtained. Israel had not attained unto grace, therefore, as a result of their doctrine of works unto righteousness their hearts were hardened or blinded.

The Greek word is *poroo,* and it means to harden, make hard like a stone, to be callous and insensitive. The national Jews had become spiritually hardened to the gospel, and blinded to God's tender reaching out to them. The Jews were insensitive to gospel teaching and the truth, first when they rejected it from Christ Jesus, and then when Paul attempted to bring the gospel to them. This blindness affected their understanding as well as hardening their hearts. We can assume that God hardened the hearts of the Jews as he had done with Pharaoh and the spiritual state of the nation of Israel is very serious at this point.

The irony is, they physically beheld the Messiah in their midst and could not recognize Him they were so blind. This is the same blindness and hardness that exists today in a land that is not saved. David refers to this condition in Psalm 69 not referring to the table in their midst. That table represents the Lord in the Passover which looked forward to Calvary and their Messiah. Jesus Christ was their Passover since the first observance in Egypt before deliverance. Israel was already darkened in vision and hardened in heart as the Lord Jesus, their Messiah, hung on the cross. The table of Israel, the Passover has become a snare to Israel up to the present. By continuing the observe Passover year after year, it is a snare, a trap, and a stumbling block to the Jews by keeping them looking forward for the Messiah who was sacrificed for them in 30 A.D. The blessing that was to be conferred upon Jews for observing the Passover has become a curse.

Isiah 29 says:

> "For the Lord hath poured out upon you the spirit of deep sleep, and hath closed your eyes; the prophets and your rulers, the seers hath he covered." (Isaiah 29:10)

He continues to say their vision is like a closed book that is sealed, not bothering to try to gain access to. Such a people will not be able to read a sealed book and, therefore, cannot learn anything.

> "For I would not, brethren, that ye should be ignorant of this mystery, lest ye should be wise

in your own conceits; that blindness in part is happened to Israel, until the fullness of the Gentiles be come in," (Romans 11:25)

"...being alienated from the life of God through the ignorance that is in them, because of the blindness of their heart." (Ephesians 4:18)

The fullness of the Gentiles does not come into its fruition until the end of the 7-year Tribulation where God not only has dealt with the Jews, but will finish dealing with the Gentiles. This will be the conclusion of the 70th week of Daniel, after a long gap between the 69th and 70th weeks. The prophetic clock stopped for Israel and the world when Messiah was cut off, crucified after the 69th week. During this period, times of the Gentiles, God is calling out the church from both Jews and Gentiles. So, if Jews that are amongst Israel, respond to God's call, accept the gospel and become born-again, are saved into heavenly glory and the scales blinding their eyes fall off completely.

"But their minds, were blinded: for until this day remaineth the same vail untaken away in the reading of the Old Testament; which vail is done away in Christ. (2 Corinthians 3:14)

The vail on the hearts of the Jewish nation refers back to Isaiah 29:10-12, when God sent the blindness upon Israel. That year was around 704 B.C. so the blindness has been a reality for over 2700 years, and will not end until the fulness of the Gentiles is come in which will be at the end of the Tribulation.

That will be a glorious time when the nation of Israel receives its sight and accepts her Messiah.

> *"They shall call on my name, and I will hear them: I will say, It is my people: and they shall say, the LORD is my God."* (Zechariah 13:9)

The light of the Lord will illuminate the dark hearts of the remnant Jews and they will cry out after recognizing the Lord Jesus Christ as their Savior. They will have been saved and have complete understanding in the light of Christ Jesus.

> *"Arise. Shine; for thy light is come, and the glory of the Lord is risen upon thee. And the Gentiles shall come to thy light, and kings to the brightness of thy rising."* (Isaiah 60:1, 3)

> *"And so all Israel shall be saved: as it is written, there shall come out of Sion the Deliverer, and shall turn away ungodliness from Jacob:"* (Romans 11:26)

In 35 A.D. we have the first martyr for Christ who was stoned by the unbelieving Jews who could not stand a witness for Jesus.

> *"And they cast him out of the city, and stoned him: and the witnesses laid down their clothes at a young man's feet, whose name was Saul."* (Acts 7:58)

That was Paul (Saul) consenting to the death of Stephen. Paul then proceeded to persecute the church, sending many believers far and wide.

> *"And they were all scattered abroad throughout the regions of Judea and Samaria, except the apostles."* (Acts 8:1b)

The Jews have already rejected Christ as Luke has recorded,

*"But ye denied the Holy One and the Just,
and desired a murderer to be granted unto you."*
(Acts 3:14).

So, they felt in control to resist Stephen's attempt to bring the Jews the Gospel.

"Then there arose certain of the synagogue, which is called the synagogue of the Libertines, and Cyrenians, and Alexandrians, and of them of Cilicia and of Asia, disputing with Stephen." (Acts 6:9)

There are a few other groups, barely worth mentioning, that were harassing Paul the Apostle. The first were the Libertines. This obscure group of Jews had something of a past. When Pompey and other generals took over Israel and Jerusalem, they took hundreds of Jewish prisoners back to Italy with them and enslaved them and treated them harshly for a time. They had been let go eventually and repatriated to their own country. They opposed Stephen and were of a certain synagogue by their name. They were referred to as freedmen, liberated slaves or their descendants. They supposedly formed a colony on the banks of the Tiber River. There are many conjectures about them, more than confirmed facts. If they lived up to the name, they were licentious and demonic; not under the restraint of law or religion. One could say that as a group they were debauched.

The Cyrenians were from the African town of Cyrene, in a country we know as Libya. Founded by Greeks, it had a large number of Jews, who were brought to Cyrene by Ptolemy for security. The Jews of Cyrene grew in number and influence. Besides the Libertines having a synagogue in

Jerusalem, the Cyrenes had one as well. There was a group of Cyrenians in Jerusalem on Pentecost. They joined with the others in being violently critical of Stephen. Simon of Cyrene was also mentioned as being called on to help the Lord with the cross on crucifixion day. Lucius of Cyrene (Acts 13:1) was one of the certain prophets and teachers at Antioch, a church that was an offshoot of the Jerusalem church. According to Unger, the synagogue of the Cyrenes at Jerusalem was destroyed in the 4th century by Saracens.

The Saracens were groups of assassins for hire. The name means daggar. They roamed Palestine looking for trouble and money.

The Saracens were the military arm, among a few others, of King Agrippa.

> *"Now they which were scattered abroad upon the persecution that arose about Stephen travelled as far as Phenice (Phoenicia, modern Lebanon), and Cyprus, and Antioch, preaching the word to none but unto the Jews only.*
>
> *And some of them were men of Cyprus and Cyrene, which, when they were come to Antioch, spake unto the Grecians, preaching the Lord Jesus."* (Acts 11:19:20)

This is now 41 A.D. and the church at Antioch, the first one founded by Christians outside of Jerusalem, and became a stronghold as a major church. It was known as the first Gentile church and the one Paul was sent out from for his missionary journeys. It was a busy church with many visitors and speakers.

> *"And it came to pass, that a whole year they assembled themselves with the Church, and taught much people."* (Acts 11:26)

The Alexandrians were another group that opposed Stephen, from an ornate, beautiful town in northern Egypt in northern Africa. This concerns the Jews, who made up nearly half of the population of Alexandria, also had their own synagogue in Jerusalem.

There were those of Cilicia and of Asia who also contended with Stephen. Acts 6:10 says that all these groups together could not resist the wisdom and spirit of Stephen.

> *"And I will sow them among the people: and they shall remember me in far countries; and they shall live with their children, and turn again."* (Zechariah 10:9)

This scattering and denial of access to the land of the Jews is threatening in the middle of the first century. It is from this second scattering that the Jews are now being re-gathered back to Israel. This re-gathering will continue until the fullness of the Gentiles comes in. It is estimated that in New Testament times only about two and one-half million Jews lived in Israel, when four to six million Jews lived outside of the country.[107]

There were two main revolts or wars that the Jewish nation wages against Rome. These occurred in 66-73 A.D. and 132-135 A.D. Conditions were getting worse inside Israel due to internal problems and suppression from Rome, especially from Nero. The dispersions before the wars with Rome, led to many colonies of Jews set up in nearly every city throughout the region. Also many of the descendants of many of these Jews outside of Israel never returned. As mentioned, there were perhaps only about two and one-half million Jews living in Israel at the time of Christ. There were four to six million Jews who lived outside the country.

The Jews were scattered into regions of Mesopotamia, which was situated within the Tigris-Euphrates river system, corresponding to modern day Iraq, Kuwait, eastern Syria, southeastern Turkey and interacting border regions.[108] The Jews were also found in Syria/Asia Minor, Egypt, Italy, and North Africa. Asia Minor in Biblical Times consisted of what is modern Turkey, also known as the Anatolian peninsula or Asian Turkey. Paul established many Christian, Gentile churches there, none of which exist today. There were also colonies of Jews in Spain. The Jews were in Egypt in and around Alexandria. There were nearly 50,000 Jews living in Rome at the time. Paul got a report from Jews while at the synagogue in Jerusalem about the situation.

> *"...thou seest, brother, how many thousands of Jews there are...and they are informed of thee, that thou teachest all the Jews which are among the Gentiles to forsake Moses,"* (Acts 21:20,21)

Back in the first century A.D. the Jews mainly stuck to their beliefs but others took a more accommodating path under pressure to assimilate.

> "This people has already made its way into every city, and it is not easy to find any place in the habitable world which has not received this nation and in which it has not made its power felt." Strabo, quoted in Josephus Jewish Antiquities.

The First War of Rome

In 66 A.D. the Jews revolted against the Roman Empire. Induced by Roman rule and tyrants like Caligula and Nero, who demanded worship as gods from the Jews, and constant harassment from the revolutionary Zealots, the two sides erupted into conflict. At first the rebellion was successful, defeating the Legate of Syria and forcing him from Jerusalem. King Agrippa II fled the city to Galilee and later gave themselves (he and his wife Berenice) up to the Romans.

The history of the war is written in detail by Josephus in the historical classic, "the war of the Jews." Josephus was a Jew who was a commander of Jewish forces before deserting to the Roman camp.[109] He was captured by Vespasian, and labeled "The traitor of Jerusalem" being guilty of cowardice and duplicity.[110] His work is great history. It is a searing story of the unrelieved horror and folly, of the crimes and treacherousness of the later Hasmonean and Herodian kings of the Roman procurators, of even the most enlightened emperors, of the leaders of the insurgents, and of Josephus himself.[111]

In 68 A.D. Nero died throwing the power structure of Rome into turmoil and halting the attack on Jerusalem. This was the time of Jewish Civil War among many factions; the Sicarii, the Zealots, and Simon bar Giora of the northern rebels. Many massacres of men, women, and children took place in Jerusalem. Vespasian became emperor of Rome and sent his son Titus to deal with Jerusalem in 69 A.D.

Titus lay siege to Jerusalem and surrounded the city forcing severe pressure and hardship on the Jews, cutting food and water supplies. The Romans breached the first and second walls to the city. After entering the gate, the Romans set the upper and lower city aflame and proceeded to destroy the temple. Jesus had prophesied:

> *"Seest thou these great buildings" there shall not be left one stone upon another, that shall not be thrown down."* (Mark 13:2)

Josephus offered an eyewitness report:

> "It was so thoroughly laid even with the ground by those that dug it up to the foundation, that there was left nothing to make those that came thither believe Jerusalem had ever been inhabited." (The Wars of the Jews, Book VII, Chapter 1.1)

A terrible fact emerged during the destruction of the temple. Titus, it was assumed, fought to save the Holy of Holies himself. However, his own soldiers, reports Josephus, roused to madness by the stubborn resistance, got insanely greedy of the gold and treasures contained within. They tore everything apart for the treasure. Then the whole temple was set ablaze. Josephus claims that 1.1 million Jews died in the siege of Jerusalem. But many dispute that figure. Tacitus, another historian of the time, writes that 1,197,000 Jews were killed or sold as slaves.[112]   Any born-again Jews or Gentiles were long gone to be scattered among the nations and none happened to be counted as dead or captured.

Bar-Kochba Revolt

In 132 A.D. Bar Kokhba led a rebellion against Hadrian; the revolt and resulting loss led to the renaming of Jerusalem as Aelia Capitoliva. Following the Bar Kokhba revolt Jews were reduced to being a wholly Diaspora people.

Due to growing tensions in Israel following the first war, namely a large military presence in Judea, the construction of Aelia Capitoliva over Jerusalem's ruins, and the building of a pagan temple to Jupiter on the temple mount, all provoked the uprising. It was the emperor Hadrian, who promised to rebuild the temple but then proceeded to build a temple dedicated to his god, Jupiter upon the ruins of the destroyed Jewish Temple in Jerusalem.

The revolt was led by Simon bar Kokhba and Elasar, and quickly spread nearly conquering Jerusalem. There were several phases to the revolt, including building of a defense system of hideout caves and many houses with underground hideouts. The forces of Bar Kokhba after suffering severe losses in the summer of 135 A.D., and breached at the fortress of Betar, were destroyed. The Jerusalem Talmud relates that the number of dead in Betar was enormous. The Romans went on killing until their horses were submerged in blood to their nostrils.[113] According to Cassius Dio, 580,000 Jews were killed in the 4-year war.[114] The Bar-Kokhba revolt saw the almost total destruction of the Jewish communities of Alexandria, where they comprised a quarter of that great city's population, and the decimation of all Jewish communities in North Africa and Cyprus.[115]

92 Reese. "Chronological Bible." 1977. p 1248

93 Osterley. "History of Israel." p 184

94 Oesterley. "History of Israel." p 185

95 Ibid.

96 Rice, Edwin. "Out Sixty-Six Sacred Books." P 112

97 Cloud. "Way of Life Encyclopedia." pp 23, 24.

98 Ibid. p 23

99 Schonfield. "History of Biblical Literature." p 148

100 Ibid. p. 148

101 Enns. "Moody H.B. of Theology." p 222

102 Ibid.

103 Stoner, "Science Speaks." Accessed through Josh.org.

104 Conwell." O.T. Predictions of Coming Messiah"

105 Smith's Bible Dictionary. "Nazarene." p 215

106 Stephen Chitty. Journeys." p 3

107 Philo, "Legatio and Caium." 36. thetransformedsoul.com

108 Wikipedia. "Mesopotamia."

109 Schweitzer. "History of Jews Since First Century A.D." p 34.

110 Ibid.

111 Ibid.

112 International Christian Zionist Center. Diaspora II-The Scatterings.

113 Jerusalem Talmud. Ta'anit. 4.5. en.wikipedia/bar Kokhba.

114 Cassius Dio. "Roman History." Book 69.12: 1-14

115 Christian Zionist Center. Diaspora II – The Scatterings.

CHAPTER 4

LAST REMNANT – REVELATION 12

This is a book on the Remnant. It has also brought out the error of calling the Christian Church the Remnant Church. That just cannot be true in a Biblical sense. The Lord Jesus formed His Church while here on earth and told us when it would be activated.

> *"And I say also unto three, that thou art Peter, and upon this rock I will build my Church, and the gates of hell shall not prevail against it."* (Matthew 16:18)

The Church in Revelation is presented in the figure of seven churches, and they were real churches, in real locales, the ruins of which can be visited today. Once again, the Church, as a Church, is here now on earth at this very minute. Christ loves the Church and gave Himself for it. Any other definition or belief is pure nonsense, borders on blasphemy and heresy, and is an affront to Christ Himself and true believers.

The Church Has a head (Christ) over it and that could not have happened until after Christ had resurrected from the dead. It could have not happened until God:

> *"Hath put all things under his feet, and gave him to be the head over all things to the church, which is his body, the fulness of him that filleth all in all."* (Ephesians 1:22, 23)

Also, the Church could not be an operating entity with functioning spiritual gifts until after Christ's ascension.[116]

> *"Wherefore he saith, when he ascended up on high, he led captivity captive, and gave gifts unto men. For the perfecting of the saints, for the work of the ministry, for the edifying of the body of Christ:"* (Ephesians 4:8, 12)

The Bible uses the term, the Body, the Body of Christ, over and over again for the Church; never remnant. What? is not the Bible or the name Body, good enough? Its Body, Body, Body, not remnant. It seems (no, is), obvious that the Church began on Pentecost as a functioning body (the Body of Christ), with the outpouring of the Holy Spirit on that glorious day.

> *"For by one spirit are we all baptized into one body."* (1 Corinthians 12:13a)

This is Spirit Baptism and it places the believer in the Body of Christ. It does not say that Spirit baptism places a believer into the remnant or remnant church. It just doesn't. What is the Body of Christ? The Body of Christ is the Church, as we have already seen in Ephesians 1:22, 23. Therefore, the Church began, the Body, when those in Acts 2:4 were filled with the Holy Spirit and began to preach the gospel in understandable languages for all the many different nationalities and tongues of people present in Jerusalem. Christ had promised this at His ascension and this is exactly what happened.

"For John truly baptized with water; but ye shall be baptised with the Holy Ghost not many days hence."

The visible church began on Pentecost (Acts 2:42-47)

Christ is, "the head of the body, the church:" (Colossians 1:18a). In an article, an excellent paper, Dr. Moorman gives eight New Testament usages for the word Church:

1. Body
2. Building
3. House
4. Temple
5. Assembly
6. Gathering
7. Priesthood
8. Bride

The term remnant does not even rank in that eight. For sure Dr. Moorman would have used the term remnant in the first eight listing if he felt it was warranted. Perhaps it was next on his list at number nine. No, he did not use remnant as a description for the Church because remnant is not a description or term for the Church, simple as that. Once again, using the term remnant or remnant Church is so demeaning to the Lord Jesus Christ for the fact He gave His very life for it. He is performing His work in the church:

"that he might present it to himself a glorious church, not having spot or wrinkle, or any such thing; but that it should be holy and without blemish." (Ephesians 5:27)

Remnant, in definition in one place on the internet, defines it as such: a small minority of people who will remain faithful to God and so be saved (in allusion to biblical prophecies concerning Israel).

This is about the end-time remnant. It is not referring to the Age of Grace or Church Age, not the time immediately after the Rapture of the Church, but what is going to happen at the mid-point of the Tribulation, just following the Abomination of Desolation. There are many names for this particular remnant.

1. Jewish Remnant
2. Holy Remnant
3. Eschatological Remnant
4. Prophetic Remnant
5. Godly Remnant
6. Tribulation Remnant
7. Faithful Remnant

There may be many more but these will suffice for the point. Some of these names have been applied to remnant in the past, but all of these are applicable to the upcoming, future remnant. As mentioned before, the dictionary definition does not apply here. It says it is a small, remaining part, quantity, number, or the like. A fragment or scrap, a trace, vestige. As stated before, none of these terms are applied by God to the Church. The real definition or description of the Tribulation Remnant is not found in the definition of remnant at dictionary.com.

What is being sought here is the "Primary Association" of the word and how it applies to the Jewish Nation. There is no denying the secular, worldly use of the word remnant, whether you use it for a dinosaur's soft tissue or last night's meal leftovers.

According to Gerhard F. Hasel, the remnant motif applied to three groupings for remnant as found in the Bible. Hasel is of the Adventist bent, but though they may not be taken as a final authority on the remnant, some of their language portrayed some clearness of thought and definition. Even though Hasel is the "authoritative study" on the remnant, he and the Adventists are not considered anywhere near that here. For example:

> "Adventist ecclesiology cannot ignore the fact that from its beginnings, the Adventist movement saw itself as the remnant mentioned in Revelation 12:17"[117]

This is not at all possible and a heretical approach.

> "Add thou not unto his words, lest he reprove thee, and thou be found a liar." (Proverbs 30:6)

This is unfortunate since the Adventists have done some very sophisticated work about the remnant. This outlook has fueled an intense drive for their message they project to the world, their proclaiming that they have a special gospel truth to share, and it goes to nearly every foundation they build upon. They build upon their usage of the word motif, used together with remnant. A motif is the dominant idea used in artistic or literary way.

Mr. Hasel then, is the Adventists' main go to source for all the theology they have assembled on the subject of the remnant.

So, according to them, there are three distinctions or groups that the motif is applied to. The historical remnant (and this has either caught on from their usage, or Hasel has borrowed it from the domain) is any group that has come through a catastrophe of some sort, with its identity intact. The first reference to something like this is in Genesis 4:1-15. This type has no bearing or relevance on what is being discussed in this chapter.

The second type of remnant is the so-called faithful remnant. This might be a sort of community of Jews or Gentiles, exhibiting some spirituality and a faith relationship to God, but not to Jesus Christ personally. An example of this type may be found in Genesis 7:23 in reference to Noah and his family referred to loosely as a righteous remnant. This group serves no purpose here either.

The third group is called the eschatological remnant. Eschatological, according to the online dictionary.com; is relating to death, judgment, and the final destiny of the soul and of humankind. This fits our narrative here pretty well, that is Tribulation times. There will be many deaths in the first 3.5 years of the Tribulation leading to the time of the remnant. The entire seven-year Tribulation is a time of judgment: judgment of the Gentiles and judgment of the Jews. Surely the final destiny of all souls and humankind will also be determined at that time.

This eschatological end-time is part of theology concerned with the final events of the history of our time, and about the ultimate destiny of humanity. This will be about the end-time, and the end-time Jewish remnant that will be in the safe hands of God while death and utter destruction of the world is all around.

So, the eschatological remnant will be the ones in Israel who will come out of the fires of persecution, perpetrated on them by a false Christ, the Antichrist. When they turn to the Lord Jesus Christ, they will be the heirs to the Kingdom of God.

> *"The sun shall be turned into darkness, and the moon into blood, before the great and the terrible day of the LORD come.* (Joel 2:31)

Since this time and this chapter occurs during the Tribulation found in the book of Revelation, it is profitable to examine briefly four views of Revelation that are out there. These are: 1) Preterist; 2) Idealist; 3) Classical Dispensationalist; 4) Progressive Dispensationalist.

Preterist

The Preterist has his/her in the past interpretations for certain Scriptures and turns around and questions futurists' claims as not being made in confidence.

One such Scripture that really throws them for a loop is what Jesus was saying about the time of His coming. They suppose that He said that He would return in that first century generation, before, *"there be some standing here, which shall not taste of death."* (Matt. 10:23; Matt.27, 28) Then they ask, "did you ever wonder why the first century Christians expected Jesus to come in their lifetime, and how they got that expectation?" The next chapter, chapter 17, contained the explanation of what the Lord meant.

This was fulfilled for the Apostles at the transfiguration of Jesus. The transfiguration is the picture of the Son of man coming in His Kingdom. Peter confirmed that in 2 Peter 1:16-18 that Jesus was glorified on that mount with three accompanying disciples, this statement from 2 Peter was fulfilled. The transformation was but a miniature of the Kingdom which Peter confirmed.

Preterists by denying this cut themselves off from being part of Christ's humanity as He is in the hope of humanity. What the Apostles saw as Christ was transfigured, is the kind of person and the way we will be some day if one is a saved child of God. (1 John 3:2). This prospect of being like Christ is our promise in the future. This is not in Preterist theology and will not be fulfilled for any person partaking in Preterism.'

Beware of Preterism which says that all biblical prophecy has been fulfilled, including the second coming of Christ, Satan and the Antichrist have been thrown already into the lake of fire, the resurrection of the dead has already taken place, and the total arrival of the Kingdom of God has come. Plus, all things have been made new, the old heaven and earth have passed away, and the new heaven and earth have come, etc.

Idealist

In Christian eschatology, Idealism (also called the Spiritual approach, the allegorical view, the non-literal view of scripture and many more) involves interpretation of the book of Revelation which sees all of the imagery of the book as symbolic. The idealist sees Revelation and its events as being carried out and fulfilled throughout the history of the Church.

This stance says that Revelation is not to be taken to mean a relation to any specific historical events which will happen in any future time frame. It only relates to spiritual truths, continuing the allegorical method of interpretation which was popular in the medieval times. This thought pattern still finds favor with those who diminish the actual events of the end-time as being actual events. It is absurd to deny to the book of Revelation, the horrible, true events that will occur to close this time period.

The millennium does not relate to the Church Age, as they say it does. To Idealists, or allegorists, the book of Revelation is a symbolic display of good versus evil. Together with Preterists, the reality of future events and, therefore, judgment of this world, is conveniently avoided. By denying any literal interpretation to any future events, they dismiss any real finality to the truth that the book of Revelation depicts God's final victory in His judging the realm of evil.

The idealist Calkins summarizes idealism: 1) it is an irresistible summons to heroic living. 2) The book (Revelation) contains matchless appeals to endurance. 3) It tells us that evil is marked for overthrow in the end. 4) It gives us a new and wonderful picture of Christ. 5) The Apocalypse reveals to us the fact that history is in the mind of God and in the hand of Christ as the author and reviewer of the moral destines of men.[118] Oh, how nice of the idealists to reduce such epic events of prophetic importance to be a mere devotional.

Classical Dispensationalist

Without having to go into a book length expose of Dispensationalism, (for example: "Dispensationalism," by Charles Ryrie), this will be brief about how it views Revelation. One thing about Classical Dispensationalism (C.D.) is that the present day Church Age is a temporary interim before the resumption of God's dealings with the nation of Israel. It also upholds the clear distinction between Israel and the Church.

We are currently in the Dispensation of Grace. God is making known His eternal program in a progressive manner, which includes His purposes for man on the earth.[119] It is based on the need to rightly divide the words of God, its process settling the right dividing of truth from the confusion bound to arise when one reads and misinterprets God's words out of their context.

In regards to the Dispensation of Grace, it is the period of time from the crucifixion, which ended the Dispensation of Law, to Christ's coming to the earth towards the end of the Tribulation, in order to fight and destroy the Antichrist forces at the battle of Armageddon.

The word dispensation means an order, economy or administration; the law of the house.[120] It is used four times in the New Testament: 1 Corinthians 9:17; Ephesians 1:10, Ephesians 3:2; and Colossians 1:25. Scofield defines it as: "A dispensation is a period of time during which man is tested in respect to obedience to some specific revelation of the will of God.[121]

"Study to shew thyself approved unto God, a workman that needeth not to be ashamed, rightly dividing the word of truth." (2 Timothy 2:15)

That is the goal of Classic Dispensationalists in rightly dividing the word of God.

Dr. A.C. Gaebelein commented on the subject:

> "there has always been an outcry against the dispensational truths, as revealed in the word of God, from the side of post-millennialists and modernists."[122]

Progressive Dispensationalism

Dr. Craig Blaising and Dr. Darrell Bock, two Dallas Theological Seminary professors have put out a book questioning previous righty divided truths of Dispensationalism. It is written in a very dense, erudite, technical style, totally the opposite of the clear, direct, and concise scholarship of the writers of Dispensationalism (Classic). These P.D. writers, it would seem, are in the perceived process of destroying Classic Dispensationalism. At its best, within Dispensationalism has always been a dynamic that drives it to be constantly correcting itself in the light of Scripture.[123]

One tenet of P.D. is that Christ is now reigning (spiritually) on David's throne. This clashes with the settled idea that Christ ascended to the right hand of the Father's throne and will during the Millennium have left the Father's side to reign literally on David's throne throughout. Since those of P.D believe that Christ is on David's throne there is now the unanticipated fulfillment of the Davidic Covenant. They are in the habit of using a dialectical phrase "already/not yet" to support a form of realized eschatology.[124] If one is not a Dispensationalist then the present Church Age is seen as a realized form of the Millennial Kingdom. That is, they (P.D.'s) see that the Kingdom (to be in the future) is both present and future at the same time. This conjures up an illustration that is just an absurd depiction of Catdog.

There is definitely a dialectical approach employed by the P.D. authors (theologians!) to blend together elements of contradictory ideas. This can be confusing to Christians and they need a strong suggestion to get off the pot. There is either a precept, a prophecy, or a truth that is fulfilled or it isn't fulfilled. The fact is, Classic Dispensationalism has found its identity in what is absolutely essential for it to be the quintessential form of Bible interpretation.

Selah

"He slew of Edom in the Valley of salt ten thousand, and took Selah by war, and called the name of Joktheel unto this day." (2 Kings 14:7)

Selah is from *sela*, which designates sela. It is used as "rock" in Judges 1:36, "And the coast of the Amorites was from the going up to Akrabbim, from the rock, and upward." Selah is a real place, literal place, and exists still today. The word selah, used in 2 Kings 14:7, shows the geographic location of the place we call Petra today. Strong's defines sela, as the rock city of Idumea, a city in Edom; both of them describe Petra.

Petra is a site in Jordan's southwestern desert. It is accessed through a narrow canyon called Al Siq, with different style buildings carved right into the reddish-pink sandstone cliffs. Petra is also a word meaning stronghold. In the time of Christ, Petra was booming as it is now, except nowadays it is because of tourism. The only entrance is through that one long defile (a steep-sided narrow gorge or passage. Sela Petra or sela is mentioned in Isaiah 16:1 and as the "inhabitants of the rock: in Isaiah 42:11:)

> *"Let the wilderness and the cities thereof lift up their voice, the villages that Kedar doth inhabit: let the inhabitants of the rock sing, let them shout from the top of the mountains."*

Obadiah must have had Petra and its inhabitants in mind directly when he prophesied to Edom:

> *"The pride of thine heart hath deceived thee, thou that dwellest in the clefts of the rock, whose habitation is high;"* (Obadiah 3)

The Jews, during their near 2000 years of their dispersion have been constantly in need of a hiding place. In these very last days, when they now have returned to the land, will need a very special and particular hiding place.

> *"Alas! For that day is great, so that none is like it: it is even the time of Jacob's trouble; but he shall be saved out of it."* (Jeremiah 30:7)

Satan will make his last and final ditch effort to eradicate the Jews, and a most likely hiding place God will direct them to will be the ancient city of Esau, Petra.

This time of Jacob's trouble, the Tribulation, will be a time of very fierce persecution and not a time of peace. The time will be so troublesome for the Jews that they cannot see a way out.

> *"And in that day will I make Jerusalem a burdensome stone for all people*: (Zechariah 12:3a)

> *"For I will gather all nations against Jerusalem to battle; and the city shall be taken, and the houses rifled, and the women ravished; and half of the city shall go forth into captivity, and the residue of the people shall not be cut off from the city."* (Zechariah 14:2)

To have open eyes is to see the Jews will be forced to get out, those who can, of Jerusalem and flee to a place in the wilderness, which so happens to also be in the mountains. Petra becomes more important for the reasons:

1. It was a water source in the midst of a desert region.
2. It is situated in a valley surrounded by almost impassable mountains and cliffs, with the only entrance a narrow gorge, which is defendable.
3. Its colorful sandstone cliffs were perfect for carving elaborate habitats.
4. It was an ideal trade and commerce post.[125]

The unusual coloring of the stone cliffs and building façade is due to iron and silica reacting to either the heavy winter rainfall, or upward seepage from the underground water source in the area. The sandstone will change colors from yellow, to red, to pink, and various hues in between as the sun moves from east to west across the sky.[126]

If the nation of Israel, as now constituted is to be preserved until the end of the Tribulation, a hiding place will be required for the remnant. It is a world-wide effort during the Tribulation that will come after Israel and the Jews. The Antichrist will be in power and there will be a point where there will be no place for the Jews to hide except for the one God has prepared for them, and protect them in order for them to reach it.

> "Come, my people, enter thou into thy chambers, and shut thy doors about thee: hide thyself as it were for a little moment, until the indignation be overpast." (Isaiah 26:20).

The indignation that Isaiah writes about is the same as the "abomination" that the Antichrist will commit. Israel can be hidden during the last half of the Tribulation in the chambers of Petra until the Lord comes for them.

There are thousands of caves in Petra and the entire area abounds in natural caverns.[127] The remnant Jews will flee to Selah Petra and be safe there for the 3.5-year period of "indignation" until they are freed.

Tribulation

The present condition of Israel in regard to their religious faith is on life support. The faith of nearly all Israel is neither true Judaism nor Christianity. There are more non-practicing Jews and Atheists than ever. Very few are born-again believers in the Lord Jesus Christ or realize He is their Saviour. The prophet Hosea saw far in the future and stated about Israel's condition: "For the children is Israel shall abide many days without a king, and without a prince, and without teraphim:" (Hosea 3:4) The Jews have been suffering for a long time, and their plight had been prophesied by Moses before he died.

> "and is shall come to pass, that as the Lord rejoiced over you to do you good, and to multiply you; so the Lord will rejoice over you to destroy you, and to bring you to naught; and ye shall be plucked from off the land whither thou goest to possess it."

> "And the Lord shall scatter thee among all people, from the one end of the earth even unto the other; and there thou shalt serve other gods, which neither thou nor they fathers have known, even wood and stone."

> And among these nations shalt thou find no ease, neither shall the sole of thy foot have rest: but the Lord shall give thee there a trembling heart, and failing of eyes, and sorrow of mind:"

> "And thy life shall hang in doubt before thee; and thou shalt fear day and night, and shalt have none assurance of thy life:"

> "In the morning thou shalt say, would Got it were even! And at even thou shalt say, would God it were morning! For fear of thine heart wherewith thou shalt fear, and for the sight of thine eyes which thou shalt see." (Deuteronomy 28: 63-67).

It has been 72 years since Israel became a nation again on May 14, 1948. Many people think that the re-gathering and restoration of Israel being back in the land was a mistake. Being judged as a nation when Jerusalem was destroyed in 70 A.D. and then scattered to the four winds of the earth, would be enough for the whole nation to repent and get right with the Creator. There is judgment waiting at the doorstep again as Israel's apostasy will be judged in the last half of the Tribulation. Only a certain amount will escape the Antichrist.

The return of unregenerate Israel to her land is necessary and planned in order for Daniel's 70th week to come about. The Temple must be rebuilt, and all must be in place when Jesus returns so that Israel can recognize who they have pierced.

> *"And I will bring you out from all people, and will gather you out of the countries wherein ye are scattered, with a mighty hand, and with a stretched out arm, and with fury poured out."* (Ezekiel 20:34)

As the Jews were returning to their land, some promises began to be fulfilled. Where it had been a dried up and barren, desolate land since 70 A.D., rainfall amounts increased and there developed in Israel the most efficient irrigation system in the world.

Politically, Israel refuses to give up any more of their God-given land. They have survived wars and have research and development in all fields of endeavor that is the envy of the world. Today most Jews still reject Jesus Christ as Messiah. The stage is now set for the coming Tribulation and the New Israel.

Rapture

The rapture of the Church on earth is imminent. That means it will happen at any time. Christians are readying themselves for the soon gathering together with the Lord Jesus Christ in the clouds.

> *"For the Lord himself shall descend from heaven with a shout...and the dead in Christ shall*

rise first: then we which are alive and remain shall be caught up together with them in the clouds...to be with the Lord. (1 Thessalonians 4:16, 17)

"In a moment, in the twinkling of an eye,(1 Corinthians 16:52)

The Church, all the Gentiles and all the Jews who have genuinely received the Lord Jesus Christ as their Lord and Saviour, will be removed from the earth and be gone. Harpazo is the Greek word for caught up, snatched away. The Church will be snatched away and it will take place in less than a second, in the twinkling of an eye.

"...behold, a door was opened in heaven: and the first voice which I heard was as it were of a trumpet talking with me; which said, come up hither, and I will shew thee things which must be hereafter." (Revelation 4:1)

Poof! The Church, Christians and born-again Jews will be gone, opening the way for Antichrist to appear and the Tribulation and Judgment of the earth to begin.

"Let no man deceive you by any means; for that day shall not come, except there comes a falling away (departure) first, and that man of sin be revealed, the son of perdition." (2 Thessalonians 2:3)

70th Week of Daniel

The 70th week of Daniel begins with the signing of the one-week covenant (one week equals seven years) that the Antichrist signs with a spiritually blind Israel. (Daniel 9:27) According to Daniel 9:26, at the end of 69 weeks the Messiah would be cut off (crucified), and Jerusalem and the

Temple would be destroyed after that. That did happen in 70 A.D. '...and the end thereof shall be with a flood." (Dan. 9:26). It is prophesying the end of the seventy weeks. But Gabriel, when he gave Daniel the prophecy, indicated there would be a breach; the Diaspora of the Jews, known also as the Dispensation of Grace. This breach has been in place since the Messiah was killed in 32 A.D. or so.

"And he shall confirm the covenant with many for one week.": (Daniel 9:27a)

The "he" in V27 is the prince described in the verse before, who is the prince of the Roman Empire.[128] "And the people of the prince that shall come shall destroy the city and the sanctuary;" (Dan. 9:26b). Just as Titus was a prince of the Roman Empire, even so the Antichrist will be a prince of the Revived Roman Empire.[129]

The cutting off (killing) of Jesus Christ and the destruction of the Temple and Diaspora of the Jews that is at or right after the 69th week ends, picks up straight into the Tribulation at the beginning of the 70th week prophecy of Daniel, with the signing of the Antichrist Covenant with Israel. As soon as the Antichrist inks the contract for 7 years the seventieth week of Daniel, and God's prophetic clock will begin. There will be a measure of peace built up between Israel and the Antichrist, all the while the seals are opened and judgment reigns on all sides. There is a Gentile one world church growing at this time. Daily sacrifices are even allowed to be offered. God intervenes in an all-out attack on Israel by Russia and her allies, with the invading armies being wiped out supernaturally.

> "And I will turn thee back, and leave but the sixth part of thee, and will cause thee to come up from the north parts,... thou shalt fall upon the mountains of Israel," (Ezekiel 39:2,4)

From the destruction and pain of the first six seals unleashed on the evil of the earth, they cry out in anguish:"

> "For the great day of his wrath is come; and who shall be able to stand?" (Revelation 6:17).

After these opening events of Revelation and God's wrath, four angels hold back the judgments long enough to seal the 144,000 who bring the message of salvation. There are 12,000 from each of the Jewish tribes and when they are done they appear before the throne and the Lamb of God will feed them.

Of This Remnant

This coming, last end-time remnant will be different than all the others. First of all, whatever Jew that becomes a born-again Christian and is genuinely saved is still upholding the nation of Israel as did all the historical remnants. The difference is that before the very end-time remnant is to be called, the saved Jews have to be raptured with the saved Gentiles, up to the clouds to meet the Lord in the air.

For there is yet to be a Jewish remnant, and the Tribulation will be a strong witness that God has not cast away his people. This future remnant of

249

believing Jews has yet to be and will be called as soon as the Church is removed.

> *"What then? Israel hath not obtained that which he seekest for; but the election hath obtained it, and the rest were blinded."* (Romans 11:7)

Two things are going on here. God is still calling out His church, and He is reserving the Post-Rapture remnant from being revealed. Then God will remove his Church. If it were true that the Church was going through the Tribulation, God forbid, for we look for that Blessed Hope, then it would be equally true to have a saved Jewish National Congress of believers now. That would be most acceptable to many today, that is for sure, but it would produce a double testimony that fails to be in one accord with any of God's Dispensational teachings.

This Revelation remnant will be given the gospel of the Kingdom which will be centered in Jerusalem and go out to all nations during the Tribulation.

> *"And this gospel of the kingdom shall be preached in all the world for a witness unto all nations; and then shall the end come."* (Matthew 24:14)

Refer to the section in the Introduction on the gospels for an explanation of the gospel of the kingdom. The 144,000 sealed Israelites, representing each Jewish tribe, will be the preachers whom God uses during the Tribulation to form a believing remnant. The 144,000 are not this particular remnant, for they are raptured out and we find them before the throne of God.

> *"And he said to me, these are they which came out of great tribulation,…Therefore, are they before the throne of God, and serve him day and night in his temple:"* (Revelation 7: 14, 15)

We read that Israel was cut off during the Diaspora, the dispersion,"…the fig tree shall not blossom, neither shall fruit be in the vines; the labor of the olive shall fail…" (Habakkuk 7:17).

In these latter days, Scripture addresses Israel in the Tribulation; and in the Kingdom.

> *"Now learn the parable of the fig tree; when the branch is yet tender, and putteth forth leaves,…when he shall see all these things, know that it is near,…"* (Matthew 24: 32,33)

Any kind of teaching about a Jewish remnant in these end times, or be as the apostolic remnant in the beginning of the Dispensation of Grace is impossible.

It is not possible to be teaching that a Jewish remnant is or has been forming for such a time as this. There cannot be the attempt to form Jewish believing assemblies, continuing as Jews by trusting in Christ and circumcising, holding fasts for feast days, or using Jewish customs, marrying the doctrines of grace and the Church which is His Body.

The believing Jew at this time is not "gentilized," as has been pressed so much from certain sides, but he becomes a member of the Body of the Lord Jesus Christ, and has with every other believer a heavenly hope, a heavenly destiny."[130] The saved disciples spoke to Paul about what he had preached to Jews:

> "And they are informed of thee, that thou teachest all the Jews which are among the Gentiles to forsake Moses, saying that they ought not to circumcise their children, neither to walk after the customs." (Acts 21:21)

But then the Holy Spirit addressed an Epistle to the Hebrews,...it also reveals how the Holy Spirit shows them the better things of the New Covenant.[131] Hebrews shows Jews the better priest, a priest after the order of Melchizidek. Being shadows of better things, according to Hebrews, all ceremonies, all Levitical observances, are to be discontinued.

Further Tribulation

Israel suffers the beginning judgment in the first six seals that bring wrath upon the earth. This is into the 70th week of Daniel. It begins with a covenant signed with the Antichrist for a period of seven years. The first seal depicts the Antichrist's white horse going forth to conquer all (Rev. 6:2). The red horse spreads war on the earth where untold numbers of people will be killed. The black horse of famine and economic collapse rides out next as the third seal is opened. The pale horse of death and hell rides out, the fourth seal, as multitudes of the dead and unsaved are turned into hell. A fourth of all the earth's population was now gone, at least two-and-a-quarter billion people are killed. The fifth seal concerns the saved masses out of the Tribulation. The sixth seal is terrifying as a great earthquake nearly destroys the inhabitable earth. Terrified leaders hope for death to avoid, "... the great day of wrath is come." (Revelation 6:17)

The Antichrist is about to confront Israel:

> *"And in the midst of the week he shall cause the sacrifice and the ablation to cease, and for the overspreading of abominations he shall make it desolate,..."* (Daniel 9:27)

> *"When ye therefore shall see the abomination of desolation, spoken of by Daniel the prophet, stand in the holy place, whoso readeth, let him understand:"* (Matthew 24:15)

The Antichrist turns on the Jews who refuse to acknowledge him as Messiah. Matthew 24:16-21 tells of a future (maybe not so far future) time when the Jews will suddenly, all of a sudden and with great urgency, have to flee for their lives. The abomination of desolation will herald, (in the midst of the week), the last half of the Tribulation. Jewish sacrificial worship will have been reinstated. But Antichrist will shatter the holiness of the holy place:

> *"so that he as God sitteth in the temple of God, shewing himself that he is God."* (2 Thess. 2:4)

This desolate act takes place at the middle of the Tribulation. The sacrifice of the Jews in the Holy Place will abruptly come to an end. The countdown begins of 1250 days (Jewish 360 days/year)) until the Lord comes and the terrible reign of the Antichrist is ended.

"And there was given unto him a mouth speaking great things and blasphemies; and power was given unto him to continue forty and two months (3-1/2 years).

The ultimate abomination was to defile the Holy Place with sinful flesh. That place is reserved only for the Lord Jesus Christ. The High Priest, or anyone who entered therein without blood was instantly killed. The Antichrist will enter the Holy of Holies, claim to be the true Messiah and for it receives a grievous wound which he will survive. He will counterfeit the atonement and offer his image that he will say was offered in atonement and kill anybody who refuses to worship him as God.

Anyone who refuses to worship the Antichrist after he proclaims to be God will be made desolate. The last half of the Tribulation is, therefore, turned into one great war on earth.

> *"And unto the end of the war desolations are determined."* (Daniel 9:26)

> *"For then shall be great tribulation, such as was not since the beginning of the world to this time, no, nor ever shall be."* (Matthew 24:21)

So, God says, that when the abomination of desecration takes place, and Antichrist cuts off the daily sacrifice, and drives the Jews from the Temple, that is the signal,

> *"Then let them which be in Judea flee into the mountains: Let him which is on the rooftop not come down to take anything out of his house: Neither let him which is in the field return back to take his clothes. And woe unto them that are with child, and to them that give such in those days! But pray he that your flight be not in winter, neither on the Sabbath day:"* (Matthew 24: 16-20)

The distance from Jerusalem to Petra is roughly 140 miles, which was a great distance for those to travel, and elicited a cry from the remnant to God.

Psalm 44

In prophetic interpretation, Psalm 44 is the final experience of the Tribulation remnant of Israel before Jesus Christ returns for their deliverance.

> *"We have heard with our ears, O God, our fathers have told us, what work thou didst in their days, in the times of old. (V1)*

The Jews have faith in God that He will do for them what He had done for their fathers in the past. The things God did for the fathers were: drove out the heathen before them, planted Israel as a nation, He punished the heathen, they got the land for a possession, saved them by his power from harm, with his own right hand, and by the light of His countenance.

In verse 4 the remnant acknowledges God as their king. In verses 5 and 6, the remnant implores God to take revenge on their enemy, which is Antichrist and the Beast system. He will return and deliver Israel, since they are being pushed down on by the evil one.

> *"Through thee will we push down our enemies: through thy name will we tread them under that rise up against us. (V5)*

In verse 6 Israel pledges their trust in God and not in ordinary weapons. The revenge they seek is justified under the law which will be their right. It is the same with us as it was with the Jews. We are to not avenge our own selves, but pray to God to save people and to clear obstacles to the gospel that are in the way. Faced with the insurmountable the best thing for the remnant and us to do is turn to God to take care of the situation whatever it may be. It is not wise to discredit anyone that does not deserve it, for you discredit God in their eyes.

These are the Jewish remnant saints and Antichrist is out to overcome them and they need God's help. They can't fight back, they refused the Mark of the Beast and they will all be killed if God does not intervene.

In verses 9 through 16 is the list of the grievances that Israel is responsible for but always blamed God for. They had been hated by their enemies, slaughtered, scattered among the heathen, sold into slavery, robbed, scorned and derided. But they had rebelled continually against God and refused to keep his laws. (Leviticus 26: 16-45)

> "For the voice of him that reproacheth and blasphemeth; by reason of the enemy and avenger." (Psalm 44:16)

They (the Jews), in times past, blamed their enemies for their own national apostasy. They proceeded to blame God too.

> "All this is come upon us; yet we have not forgotten thee, neither have we dealt falsely in thy covenant." (verse 27)

They were proven unfaithful to the covenant God made to Moses. That made it imperative that that the Jews be obedient to God's law.

The declaration of innocence shrouds a frustration from all the affliction and doubt cast on the would-be believers. From the cries of all the curses that have come upon them, they still project a state of bleary blindness to their own condition. Hence, the bragging on their part that they have not forgotten God (V17), they haven't dealt falsely with the Mosaic Covenant (V17), turned not back in their hearts (V18), declined their steps from God's ways (V18), nor forgotten the name of God (V20), and lastly, not stretched out their hands to idols (V20).

For all that lamenting God knows what they have done and all the hiding of the secrets of the heart. We cannot get away with this kind of conduct ourselves with God. They somehow deserved to be broken and covered with the shadow of death (V19). There has to be some reason they are counted as sheep for the slaughter and killed all the day long. We are guilty of painting such false pictures of God's just dealings and proven to be untrue.

It is true that the remnant is being persecuted here.

> "Yea, for thy sake are we killed all the day long, we are counted as sheep for the slaughter. (V22)

> "Awake why sleepest thou, O Lord? Arise, cast us not off forever. (V23)

Whatever gave them the idea that God was asleep? No, God sleeps not, it is not something we have to ask God to do. The remnant feels this way because they need deliverance and they need it now. They still feel cast off like their enemies, but God is in the very process of delivering them to safety. The remnant pleads for God to show them His face and be merciful to them another time around. He has not forgotten this affliction. The Hebrew, *ra*, has the meaning of bad, evil, calamity, grief, sorrow, etc. God has every intention of relieving their sufferings and afflictions. He regulates it according to his law.

> *"Thou feedest them the bread of tears; and giveth them tears to drink in great measure."* (Psalm 80:5).

The remnant, during the Tribulation, cries out for redemption and mercy. Since the Church is not here on earth during the Tribulation, Satan turns his attack on the nation of Israel. This is the Tribulation remnant that God will prepare for the fulfillment of all Israel's covenants and promises. They have been called, in the midst of the Tribulation.

> *"And it shall come to pass, that whosoever shall call on the name of the Lord shall be delivered: for in Mount Zion and in Jerusalem shall be deliverance, as the Lord hath said, and in the remnant whom the Lord shall call."* (Joel 2:32)

Revelation 12

> *"Esaias also creith concerning Israel, though the number of the children of Israel be as the sand of the sea, a remnant shall be saved:"* (Romans 9:27)

In the continuation of the prophetic visions that Christ Jesus gave John, he witnesses the historic and prophetic events which Satan tries to prevent the birth and the crowning of the Messiah as King of Kings and Lord of Lords.

"And there appeared a great wonder in heaven; a woman clothed with the sun, and the moon under her feet, and upon her head a crown of twelve stars: and she being with child cried, travailing in birth, and pained to be delivered." (Revelation 12:1,2)

The Sun Clothed Woman

Who is this woman? Rome thinks she is the queen of heaven, found in Jeremiah, or Mary herself, who brought forth Christ. The Protestants say the woman is the visible church and the child is the true church. But that would mean the Church would be keeping the law." ...which keep the commandments of God(Rev. 12:17b). According to Deuteronomy 32:11-12; Exodus 19:4, and Revelation 12:14 the woman is Israel. The Preterists and the Reformed Covenant theology make out of the woman to be the Church. Other cultic groups make out the woman to be whatever fits their theology.

According to Genesis 37:9 in one of the dreams of Joseph, he beheld the sun and the moon and eleven stars obeying him. The eleven stars plus Joseph represented the twelve sons of Jacob, who were the head of the twelve tribes of Israel. If that is so, then the sun and the moon must represent the nation of Israel. The whole supernatural image is screaming out that it is Israel.

"And there appeared another wonder in heaven; and behold a great red dragon,..." (Rev 12:3)

Who is the red dragon? The dragon is identified in Revelation 12:3 as another, the second, wonder in heaven that appeared to John. It had seven heads and ten horns, and seven crowns upon his heads. "And the great dragon was cast out, that old serpent, called the Devil, and Satan, which deceiveth the whole world:" (Revelation 12:9). So, the wonder of the dragon is certainly, and for sure, the Devil.

The word "wonder" is more often used in conjunction with other words with similar meaning like "signs and wonders" or "miracle and wonders." The word *semeion,* could more or less mean "a sign."[132]

The birth of Christ was prophesied in Genesis 3:15. It was also prophesied that He would be virgin born, in which town He was going to be born in and that He would be born into the tribe of Judah. It was foretold by the prophets that Christ would perform miracles, that He would be killed on a cross, and His death would atone for the sins of the world. He would die, be buried, and be resurrected on the third day.

The verses say that Satan was planning to kill the Messiah soon after he was born. Jesus died on the cross instead, was raised from the dead, and ascended into heaven to be with the Father, safe from the clutches of the old dragon. Revelation 19:15 tells of His second coming, "...he should smite the nations; and he shall rule them with a rod of iron:"

Israel says:

> "Come and let us return unto the Lord,...and he will bind us up. After two days (two thousand years) will he revive us; in the third day (third millennium) he will raise us up..." (Hosea 6:1-2)

From 2007 on there were mounting joys on so-called discoveries of signs in the heavens that were said to tell humankind who knows what fantastic revelations. Around 2011 something astonishing was announced that was about to happen. On September 23, 2017, it was predicted that an astronomical alignment of starts and planets would be so arranged, over Israel (!) that seemingly would fulfill, get this, a literal word-for-word reading of Revelation 12:1-2 and Revelation 12:5! On September 23, 2017: visible over Israel the constellation Virgo (which represents a virgin woman), lying prone, becomes clothed with the sun as the sun hovers over the constellation. The new moon rests just below her feet Her head, which is always crowned by the nine fixed stars of the constellation Leo, becomes crowned with the three "wandering stars" of Venus, Mercury, and Mars to make a crown of 12 starts, etc., etc., you get a picture. What did it mean in 2017?

Michael Svigel, Dallas Theological Seminary scholar states extensively that the sign in Revelation 12 was originally the pre-eminent symbol of the pre-tribulation rapture of the Church. He also stated that the male child has a corporate meaning – it is the collective Body of Christ and cites First Corinthians 12:12.

The sign or wonder caught the eye and the pen of another evangelical, Dr. Douglas Woodward. S. Douglas Woodward is an author, speaker, and a researcher. He acknowledges that he wasn't raptured on September 23, 2017, in an article titled, "Who Revelation 12's Male Child is and Why it Matters," in the October 2017 issue of Southwest

Church's Prophetic Observer. He's trying to figure out what the "great sign" in the sky, or better yet, what the "great sign" in Revelation 12 means.

He believes that there is a reason that Revelation 12:1, 2 was highlighted at that particular time in 2017. His and his cohorts (Gary Huffman) conclusion? The "great sign" of Revelation 12 teaches that the rapture of the Church happens at least 3-1/2 years (1,260 days) before the visible return of Christ. Whoa! Doug, are those twelve hundred and sixty days based on our calendar days, or the Jewish calendar days of 30 days/month? He had better recalculate or he just might miss the "visible return" of the Lord Jesus Christ. No, no matter how you twist and convolute the Scripture the Rapture and the return of Jesus Christ to the earth happen 7 years apart, not 3-1/2 years apart.

Then, if that wasn't enough, Doug says he supplied evidence in the Southwest Church article, from several excellent sources no less, "that the male child of Revelation 12 is both Christ and the Church – the united head and body of the Church in its mystical union." He also throws in, as a side light, that Israel is the woman – an interpretation, he says, is seldom debated among scholars today. Please tell that to the Catholic scholars today.

Well, I got his email and I decided to get more insight on our differing views. In part I wrote:

> It took me at least four days to decipher the article you wrote that appeared in the Prophetic Observer for October 2017 about the man-child of Revelation 12:5. That's on me for I hadn't studied that part that closely before. I believe what Dr. Hutchings (Noah) has written in his book, "Revelation Today." On page 119 of his

book he states that Revelation 12 goes directly from the cutting off of Messiah, and the Jewish nation, right into the Tribulation period, just as if there was no Church age.

In Him, Dr. Charles Kriessman

Douglas Woodward's reply?

Thx for the fan mail. The Lord bless you. Hopefully whatever is causing your thinking process to take so long will get better soon.

S. Douglas Woodward.

Well, thank you Doug. I sure hope you get that understanding that Revelation 12 goes directly from the cutting off of Messiah, and the Jewish nation, into the Tribulation period, just as if there was no Church Age. Revelation, they say, can be pretty tricky.

"And the woman fled into the wilderness, where she hath a place prepared of God, that they should feed her there a thousand two-hundred and threescore days." (Verse 6)

After Christ's resurrection and ascension (the rapture of the church was not in view) we have the flight of the remnant of Israel to their hiding place at Petra for forty-two months. This remnant of the end-time can be found in Revelation 12 and Matthew 24 as the one-third of Israel who escape the atrocities of Antichrist. They have fled to the mountains and will be protected by God until Jesus returns for them after destroying the Antichrist, his prophet, and his armies. God will protect them in Petra, in Edom. "Who will bring me into the strong city? Who will lead me into Edom?" (Psalm 60:9) The strong city can be no place else but Petra. The remnant will be safe and preserved in the place they should be.

> *"The women were given two wings of a great eagle, that she might fly into the wilderness, into her place, where she is nourished for a time, and times, and half a time,"* (Verse14)

It used to be that heavy cloudbursts would flash flood the Ciq at Petra (the narrow entryway) and would catch entire caravans and groups of visitors by surprise, drowning them. Satan would surely try to drown a good amount of the end-time remnant if he could.

> *"And the serpent cast out of his mouth water as a flood after the woman, that he might cause her to be carried away in the flood."* (Verse 15)

Silly serpent, the Government of Jordan, has now built a dam there, making it more difficult to flood the Ciq.

> *"And the dragon was wroth with the woman, and went to make war with the remnant of her seed,"* (Verse 17)

That failed and the remnant was safe because it was God's plan all along to perform His purpose for the nation of Israel to be safe and to enter the kingdom with their Messiah as King.

---

[116] Bible.org. "Did Church begin in John 20:22 or Acts 2:4?

[117] Rodriguez, Angel (ed.). "Remnant" p 21

[118] Thomas ICE. "What is Preterism?"

[119] Keen. "The Seven Dispensations. p 3

[120] Ibid. p 4

[121] Ibid. p 4

[122] Ibid. p 6

[123] ICE. "Progressive Dispensationalism." raptureready.com. p 2

[124] Ibid. p 6

[125] Hutchings. "Petra." 1983. p 4

[126] Ibid. p 5

[127] Hutchings. "Petra" p 42.

[128] Hutchings "Seventy weeks of Daniel." p 20

[129] Ibid. p 20

[130] Gaebelein. "The Jewish Question." p 28

[131] Ibid. p 27.

[132] Hutchings. "Revelation for Today." p 118

BIBLIOGRAPHY

BOOKS

Anderson, Sir Robert. "The Coming Prince." Kregal Publications. Grand Rapids, MI 1972

Benware, Paul N. "Understanding END Times Prophecy." Moody Publishers. Chicago, IL 2006

Boa, Kenneth. "Talk Thru the Old Testament." Tyndale House Publishers, Inc. Wheaton, IL 1980

Bradbury, John W. D.D. "The Sure Word of Prophecy." Fleming H. Revell Company. 1943

Brandenburg, Kent (ed). "Thou Shalt Keep Them." Pillar & Ground Publishing. El Sobrante, CA 2003

Bright, John "The Kingdom of God." Abington Press. Nashville, TN 1981

Chafer, Lewis Sperry. "Major Bible Themes. Zondervan Publishing. Grand Rapids, MI Twelfth Printing. 1980

Costella, Dennis. "The Church: Definition & Dispensational Nature." Fundamental Bible Church. Los Osos, CA 2002

Costella, Matt. "Biblical Basics for Believers." Fundamental Evangelistic Association. Fresno, CA 2002

_____ "The Greatest Enemies of the Church, in the 21st Century. Morris Publishing. Kearney, NE 2012

Couch, Mal. (ed). "A Biblical Theology of the Church." Kregal Publications. Grand Rapids, MI 1999

_____ "Dictionary of Premillennial Theology." Kregal Publications. Grand Rapids, MI 1996

Culver, Robert. "Daniel and the Latter Days." Moody Press. Chicago, IL 1977

Dake Annotated Reference Bible. Dake Finis Jennings. Dake Bible Sales, Inc. Laurenceville, GA 1991

Dettaan, Richard W. "Israel and the Nations in Prophecy." Zondervan Publishing House. Grand Rapids, MI 1977

Estep, Howard C. "Petra' The Rose Red City." World Prophetic Ministry, Inc. Colton, CA 1970

Fruchtenbaum, Arnold. "The Remnant of Israel." Ariel Ministries. San Antonio, TX 2011

Gaebelein, A.D. "The Jewish Question." 1912

Gruden, Wayne A. "Christian Beliefs." Zondervan Publishing. Grand Rapids, MI 2005

Hutchins, Noah. "Is the Antichrist Alive Today?" Bible Belt Publishing. Oklahoma City, OK 2011

_____ "Revelation For Today." Bible Belt Publishing. Oklahoma City, OK

_____ "Exploring the Book of Daniel." Hearthstone Publishing. Oklahoma, OK 1990

_____ "Romance of Romans. Hearthstone Publishing. Oklahoma City, OK 1990

_____ "The Seventy Weeks of Daniel." Southwest Church. Oklahoma City, OK 1986

Ice & Demy. "The Return." Kregal Publications. Grand Rapids, MI 1999 pp 11-55, 147-183

Jeffrey, Grant R. "Apocalypse: The Coming Judgment of the Nations." Frontier Research Publications. Toronto 1992

Juster, Dan and Intrater, Keith. "Israel, the Church, and the Last Days. " Destiny Image Publishers 2003

Kirban, Salem. "Israel, It's Coming Tragedy and Final Triumph!" Second Coming, Inc. Huntingdon Valley, PA 1991, 1993

Kriessman, Charles J. ""The Jews and Israel." Old Paths Publications Cleveland, GA, USA 2015

Kreloff, Steven A. "God's Plan for Israel." Louizeax Brothers, Inc. Neptune, NJ 1995

Larkin, Clarence. "The Book of Daniel." Rev. Clarence Larken Estate. Glenside, PA 1929

_____ "Rightly Dividing the Word."
1920

Lindsey, Hal. "The Road to Holocaust." Bantam Books. New York 1989 pp 53-78, 101-212

McClain, Dr. Alva. "Daniel's Prophecy of the 70 Weeks." Zondervan Publishing. Grand Rapids, MI 1979

McGee, J. Vernon. "Genesis. Volume I." Griffen Printing. Glendale, CA 1980 (many from Genesis to Revelation used.)

Osterley, W.O.E. "A History of Israel, Vol. 2." Oxford University Press. 1945

Newell, William R. "The Book of Revelation." Moody Press. Chicago. Undated.

Pentecost, J. Dwight. "Prophecy for Today." Discovery House Publishers. Grand Rapids, MI 1989

_____ "Things to Come." Zondervan. Grand Rapids, MI First Grand Rapids Printing. 1964

Price, Walter K. "The Coming Antichrist." Loizeaux Brothers. Neptune, NJ 1985

Radmacher, Earl. "What the Church is All About. Moody Press. Chicago 1978

Rice, John R. "Churches and the Church." Sword of the Lord Publishers. Murfreesboro, TN 1957

Richardson, Alan. "A Theological Word Book of the Bible." MacMillan Publishing Co., Inc. New York, NY 1950

Robinson, Theodore. "A History of Israel, Vol. 1." Oxford University Press. London 1951

Rodriguez, Angel (ed). "Toward a Theology of the Remnant." Biblical Research Institute. Silver Spring, MD (Adventist). 2009

Schweitzer, Frederick. "A History of the Jews since the First Century A.D." McMillan. New York, NY 1971

Showers, Renald E. "There Really is a Difference." Friends of Israel Gospel Ministry. Bellmawr, NJ 1990

Smith, George Adam. "The Book of Isaiah." Vol I, II. Harper and Brothers. New York 1927

_____ "The Book of Isaiah." Vol 2. Country Life Press. Garden City, New York 1927

Tabb, Dr. M.H. "Ruth." Gulf Coast Bible Institute. Fort Walton Beach, FL 2006 pp 45, 46.

Vanderlugt, Herbert. "God's Plan in All the Ages." Zondervan Publishing. Grand Rapids, MI 1979

Vlach, Michael J. "Has the Church Replaced Israel?" B&H Publishing Group. Nashville, TN 2010

Walvoord, John R. "The Millennial Kingdom." Zondervan Publishing. Grand Rapid, MI 1959. pp 256-275

Webber, Dr David. "Olivet to Armageddon." Southwest Church. Oklahoma, City, OK 1979

Wood, Leon J. "The Bible & Future Events." Academic Books. Grand Rapids, MI 1973 pp1-21

ARTICLES

Adeney, W.F. "Israel's Apostasy." Biblehub.com/sermons/auth/adeney/israel's_Apostasy

Bible Genesis & Geology. "Kingdom of Heaven and Kingdom of God; the Doctrinal Difference." KJVbible.org/thekingdoms. pp 1-5

Chitty, Dr. J. Stephen. "Between the Testaments." Journeys Through the Bible.

Clarke, Adam. "Commentary. Vol I." pp 93, 94, 95, 99, 104-109, 141. Abington Press. Date unknown (old)

_____ "I Love Israel." Way of Life Literature. 2017 wayoflife.org/reports/ilove-israel.

"Daniel and the Minor Prophets with Wycliffe Commentary." Iverson-Norman Associates. New York. 1975. pp 50-54

Dettaan, Richard W. "The Times of the Gentiles." Found in "Israel and the Nations in Prophecy." Richard Dettaan. Chap. 2 pp 21-29.

_____ Chapter 5. "Israel's Seventy Weeks." In "Israel and Nations in Prophecy." Zondervan 1977. pp 49-54

Drive Thru History. "Destruction of the Temple Foretold by Jesus." drivethruhistory.com.

En.wikipedia. "First Jewish-Roman War. Wikipedia. Org. 2020

Ellis, Paul. "By Which Gospel Are You Saved? The Gospel of Grace!" escapetoreality.org/gospel of grace. pp 1-2

Essex, Keith. "The Abraham Covenant." TMSJ 10/2 (Fall 1999). 191-212

Factaboutisrael.uk. "The Mystery of the Olive Tree." 2019. pp 1-4

Fructenbaumm, Arnold." Israelolgy: The Missing Link in Systemic Theology." Part 1. www.galaxie.cmarticle/cts05-2-02." pp 1-13. Accessed Dec. 2019

Gaebelein, A.C. "The Remnant-Israel's Apostasy Not Complete." pp 19-32

Ginzberg, Louis. "Abomination of Desolation." Jewishencyclopedia.com

Got Questions? "What is British Israelism?" www.gotquestions.org.

_____ "What are the Times of the Gentiles?" www.gotquestions.org/times-of-the-Gentiles. 12-23-2018

Graham, Ron. "The Assyrian Captivity." www.somplybible.com pp 1-4

Grider, Geoffrey. "The Real Prophetic Meaning of that Mysterious Word Selah." nowtheendbegins.com pp 1-16

Harris, John L. "The Day of the Lord." Shofar Illustrator. Summer, 2007. pp 52-55

Ice, Thomas. "Matthew 24: 16-20 The Command to Flee." blueletterbible.org pp 1-5

_____ "What is Progressive Dispensationalism?" The Thomas Ice Collection. raptureready.com. pp 1-12

Ironside, H.A. "Wrongly Dividing the Word of Truth. brethrenonline.org/books/ultrad. Accessed January 29. 2003

Judiasm 101. "Who Is a Jew?" jewfaq.org/whoisjew. pp 1-4

Keen, Clarence M. "The Seven Dispensations" Foundation Magazine. Jan-Feb, 2002

Knighton, Garry. "Ten Reasons Why the Nation of Israel Fell. (Apostasy)." heartofgod.org/outlines/tenreasons. N.D.

Kriessman, Charles. "Chapter 4, The Jews and Israel." Roman 11, 2015. pp 201-234

Maier, Paul L. "Not One Stone Left Upon Another." christianhistoryinstitute.org.

McCall, Thomas. "What is the Olive tree?" Levitt.com. Levitt Letter. March 2001

McGee J. Vernon. "Judgment of Judah and Jerusalem." www.oneplace.com

Missler, Chuck. "Daniel's 70 Weeks: The Precision of Prophecy." www.khouse.org/articles/2004/552. pp 2-5

Morris, Dr. Henry. "The Everlasting Gospel." Institute of Creation Research.

One For Israel. "Are Today's Jews Genetically Descended from the Biblical Israelites?" oneforisrael.org. pp 1-8

Price, Walter K. "The Coming Antichrist." Introduction. Loizeaux Brothers. 1985. pp 8-13

Ryrie, Charles. "What You Should Know About the Rapture: The Day of the Lord" Moody Press. Chicago. 3rd Printing. 1982. pp 93-106

Sandahl, Don. "The Olive Tree (Romans II)." printerfriendly.com. April 16, 2012

Shaff, Philip. "The Jewish War and the Destruction of Jerusalem A.D. 70."

Scofield, C.I. "The Times of the Gentiles, Part 1" Bibliotheca Sacra. Bsac 107:427 (Jul 1950). pp 343-355

_____ "Gospel: Four Forms of the Gospel." Notes on age 1343.

Stallard, Dr. Mike. "The Shift from Jewish Chiliasm to Christian Chiliasm in the Early Church" Baptist Bible Seminary.

Taylor, Steve. "What is the Gospel of the Kingdom?" Lakesherbible.net/articles. pp 1-2

Transformed Soul. "Intertestamental Period." thetransformedsoul.com

Vander, Laan. "Abram's Animal Ceremony in Genesis 15." anchorsaway.org.

Waite, Daniel S. "What is Truth?" The Dean Burgon Society. B.F.T. #3476-P. 2010

Waite, D.A. "Outline Talks on Bible Dispensations." B.F.T. #3078-P. August, 2002

Watts, James W. "The Remnant Theme: A Survey of New Testament Research, 1921-1977." SBTS, 1986 pp 109-119.

Webber, Dr. David F. "God's Timetable for the Last Days." Southwest Church, Oklahoma City, OK 1982. pp 41-52

_____ "God Divided the Nations." Southwest Church, Oklahoma City, OK. 1981

Wikipedia. "Khazar Hypothesis of Ashkenazi Ancestry.": en.wikipedia.org/wiki/khazar. pp 1-9

_____ "Cyrus the Great." en.wikipedia/cyrus_the_great. pp 1-5

_____ "Jewish Diaspora." en.wikipedia.org.

_____ "Dugong." en.wikipedia.org/wiki/dugong. pp 1-4

_____ Babylonian Captivity." En.wikipedia.org. pp 1-6

Williams, H.D. "Ryrie's Five Points of Literal Fulfillment of the Abrahamic Covenant Supports Premillennialism" Old Paths Publications. Articles. Date unknown.

Woodward, S. Douglas. "Who Revelation 12's Male Child Is and Why it Matters." Prophetic Observer. October, 2017. pp 1-4

INDEX

Zealots, 5, 189, 225

Zionist, 49, 50, 52, 228

Lightning Source UK Ltd.
Milton Keynes UK
UKHW020651260720
367197UK00009B/254